you fix it:
Small Appliances

R. Emerson Harris

**in association with
Clifford Seitz and Carmine C. Castellano**

ARCO PUBLISHING COMPANY, INC.
NEW YORK

Published by Arco Publishing Company, Inc.
219 Park Avenue South, New York, N.Y. 10003

Copyright © 1979 by Training Analysis and Products, Inc.

Library of Congress Cataloging in Publication Data

Harris, R. Emerson
  You fix it, small appliances.

   1. Household appliances, Electric—Maintenance and
repair—Amateurs' manuals. I. Seitz. Clifford Peter,
1912- joint author. II. Castellano, Carmine C.,
II. Title.
TK9901.H37   1978   643'.6   73-93615
ISBN 0-668-03463-7 (Paper Edition)

Printed in the United States of America

ACKNOWLEGEMENTS

Arco Publishing Company, Inc. gratefully acknowledges the cooperation and interest of a number of small household appliance manufacturers for material used in this book.

Specific thanks are given to the following manufacturers whose appliance photographs and illustrations have been used through their courtesy:

Cory Corporation, Chicago, Illinois; Hamilton Beach, Scorwill, Housewares Group, Washington, North Carolina; McGraw Edison Company, Portable Appliances, Boonville, Missouri.

Contents

INTRODUCTION   5

COFFEE MAKERS   7
  Unit Will Not Heat   8
  Coffee Boils Or Repercolates   15
  Coffee Is Weak   18
  Coffee Is Bitter   20
  Coffee Does Not Stay Warm After Brewing   21

CORN POPPERS   23
  Unit Will Not Heat   24
  Popper Overheats; Burns Corn; Will Not Shut Off   29
  Corn Will Not Pop   30

FRY PANS   31
  Unit Will Not Heat   32
  Pan Does Not Get Hot Enough   36
  Pan Overheats   37

GRIDDLES AND GRILLS   39
  Unit Will Not Heat   40
  Unit Does Not Fully Heat With Control At High Setting   45

CLOTHES IRONS, DRY   47
  Iron Will Not Heat   48

CLOTHES IRONS, STEAM   53
  Iron Will Not Heat   54
  Iron Heat Cannot Be Adjusted   55
  Iron Leaks   56
  Iron Produces Little Or No Steam   59
  No Spray Or Poor Spray   61

ELECTRIC OVEN/BROILER   63
   Oven Will Not Heat   64
   Oven Does Not Reach Maximum Temperature With
     Control At High Setting   69

BROILER/ROTISSERIE   71
   Unit Will Not Heat   72
   Broiler/Rotisserie Does Not Reach Maximum
     Temperature   74
   Unit Heats But Rotisserie Motor Does Not Operate   75

SPACE HEATER   79
   Unit Will Not Heat   80
   Unit Does Not Reach Maximum Temperature   85
   Heater Works—Blower Does Not   87

HAIR DRYER   91
   Dryer Will Not Heat And Motor Is Inoperative   92
   Heater Element Works But Motor Does Not Run   96
   Motor Runs But Dryer Does Not Heat   98
   Motor And Heater Work But Warm Air Does Not Enter
     The Hood   101

ELECTRICAL TESTING AND TEST TOOLS   103

REPAIR TOOLS   106

INDEX   108

INTRODUCTION

Many electrical appliances are discarded because they either do not work properly or they do not work at all. In many cases there is little wrong with them and they can be repaired by the home mechanic at a cost well below that of a new appliance. This book allows you to repair your small appliances by providing step-by-step procedures for solving most of the problems you will encounter.

You Fix It is different from other books because it starts with what you know—a symptom, such as: *the coffee maker won't heat* or *the iron won't produce steam*, and it takes you through a step-by-step procedure of *what to do and how to do it.*

Let's start with an example.
Symptom—Coffee Maker Won't Heat

Step 1—Look for the symptom under Coffee Makers in the Index at the back of the book. There you will find a code number and a page number (Code **1000**, page 8). Go to that page number and you will find a Fault Symptom. You will notice there are four possible causes for this fault.

The most likely cause is listed first and so on. Follow the steps or procedures given in the Initial Conditions Check List for the Fault. This is a very important step. A repair job is often undertaken when nothing is wrong simply because an essential operating requirement was overlooked, eg. using hot water.

Step 2—If the fault is verified, follow the steps indicated until the cause has been isolated.

Step 3—Carry out the step-by-step procedures for repair and checkout.

The steps are broken down into smaller steps. Only simple tools are required and there is no need to understand electrical circuits or to acquire such knowledge. You can't miss.

CAUTION

**WHEN WORKING WITH ELECTRIC-
ITY, GREAT CARE MUST BE EXER-
CISED. ONCE AN APPLIANCE RE-
PAIR IS BEGUN, NEVER PLUG THE
APPLIANCE CORD INTO THE SERV-
ICE OUTLET. DO NOT APPLY POWER
TO THE UNIT UNTIL THE REPAIR HAS
BEEN COMPLETELY CHECKED AND
ASSEMBLY COMPLETED. ALWAYS
WORK ON A DRY SURFACE. AL-
WAYS USE FACTORY AUTHORIZED
REPLACEMENT PARTS.**

CAUTION

NOTE:

Don't use this book by simply flipping through the pages to try to find an answer. Instead, pick the fault symptom, look up the symptom in the index, and follow the procedure. It's easy!

COFFEE MAKERS (Non-Submersible)

UNIT WILL NOT HEAT

FAULT SYMPTOM 1000

Possible Causes:

- Power cord defective _____ **See 1010**
- Internal wire connections are loose or broken _____ **See 1020**
- Thermostat defective or inoperative _____ **See 1030**
- Heating element defective or has failed _____ **See 1040**

Initial Conditions Check List:

a. Plug a table lamp into the power receptacle to be sure you have a live circuit.
b. Use cold water.
c. Turn switch on coffee maker to ON position.

Step 1—Fill coffee maker with cold water. Plug coffee maker into a known active house electrical outlet.

Does the water quickly come to a boil?

Yes—Fault has not been verified. An initial condition must have been overlooked.

No—Repeat procedure several times. If no change, fault has been verified. Unplug coffee maker cord and proceed to **1010.**

1010

Power cord defective

Step 1—Examine the cord set for wear. Look for breaks in the insulation and fraying where the wires enter the receptacle and appliance plug. Check the inside of appliance plug, Fig. 1B, for pitting and dark burn marks. This is caused by removing the appliance end of the plug before removing the receptacle end. This is very poor practice and should be avoided.

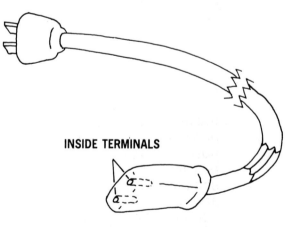

INSIDE TERMINALS

Fig. 1B. Appliance plug.

Is the cord set in good condition?

Yes—Proceed to Step 3.

No—Replace cord set with a new set and proceed to Step 2.

Step 2—Fill the coffee maker with cold water and connect the new cord set. Turn the coffee maker on.

Does the water quickly come to a boil?

Yes—Fault has been isolated and repaired.

No—Proceed to **1020**.

Step 3—Check the cord set for poor connections or breaks in the wire with a test light. Refer to Service Procedure **11000**.

Does the cord set check out OK?

Yes—Proceed to **1020**.

No—Replace the cord set and go back to Step 2.

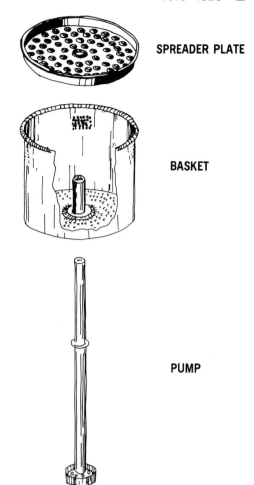

Fig. 2. Spreader plate, basket, and pump.

1020

Internal wire connections are loose or broken

CAUTION

MAKE SURE THE PLUG IS REMOVED FROM THE WALL OUTLET.

CAUTION

Step 1—Remove the top basket and pump assembly from the coffee maker, as per Fig. 2. Place the percolator in an upside down position. Remove the screw or bolt that secures the base assembly to the pot (see Fig. 3) and gently remove the base. On the inside you will find the wire lead assembly, a pilot

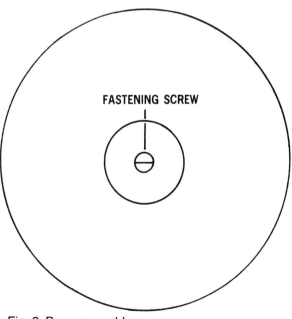

Fig. 3. Base assembly.

light, a warming heater, main heater, and the thermostat. On some models you will also find a thermostat control arm. The arrangement and supporting brackets will vary from model to model but the listed elements will be there. A typical wire arrangement is shown in Fig. 4. Two typical coffee makers are illustrated in Figs. 5 and 6.

Step 2—Inspect the wiring assembly and connectors for loose connections or broken wires.

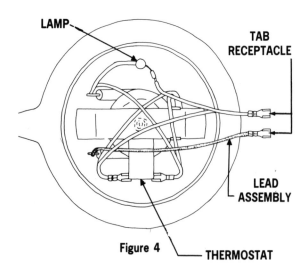

LAMP

TAB RECEPTACLE

LEAD ASSEMBLY

Figure 4

THERMOSTAT

Are there any loose connections or broken wires?

Yes—Proceed to Step 3.

No—Proceed to **1030**.

Step 3—Remove the connector by heating the connection with a soldering iron, and remove broken wire. If a mechanical connection is used, pry open the crimped edge (A) and slide out the broken wire (B), as per Fig. 7.

Remove the insulation from the disconnected wire and resolder or recrimp. If there is insufficient slack in the wire to allow a

repair, a new wire assembly should be obtained from an authorized supplier and installed. Reconnect the lead. Reassemble the percolator. Proceed to Step 4.

NOTE:

Handle the leads carefully. The insulation can be very brittle.

CAUTION

NEVER MAKE THIS REPAIR BY TWISTING WIRES TOGETHER AND TAPING.

CAUTION

Step 4—Fill the coffee maker with cold water and turn it on.

Does the water quickly come to a boil?

Yes—Fault has been isolated and repaired.

No—Proceed to **1030**.

1030

Thermostat defective or inoperative

Step 1—Remove the base assembly as described in **1020**. Proceed to step 2.

Step 2—Remove the connectors from each side of the thermostat: be gentle. See Figs. 4, 5, and 6 for identification. Attach the alligator clamp of a test light (see **11000**) to one of the terminals on the thermostat and touch the probe to the other terminal, as per Fig. 8C.

Did the test light glow?

Yes—The thermostat is OK. Proceed to **1040**.

No—The thermostat is defective and must be replaced. Proceed to Step 3.

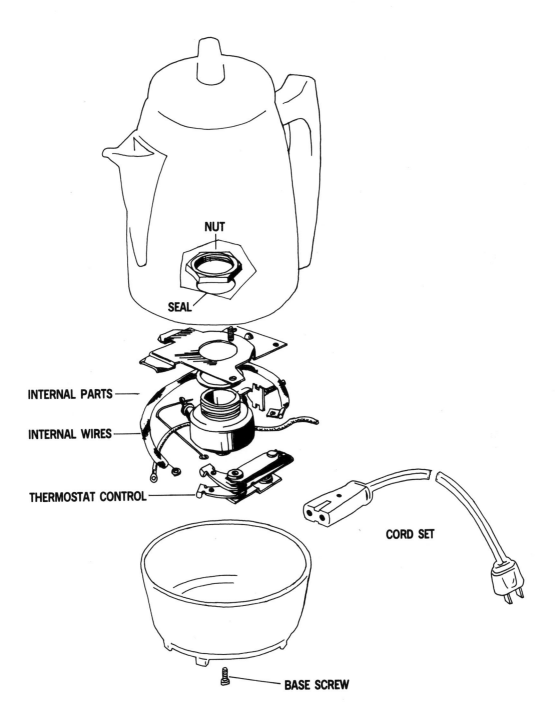

NUT

SEAL

INTERNAL PARTS

INTERNAL WIRES

THERMOSTAT CONTROL

CORD SET

BASE SCREW

Fig. 5. Typical electric coffee maker.

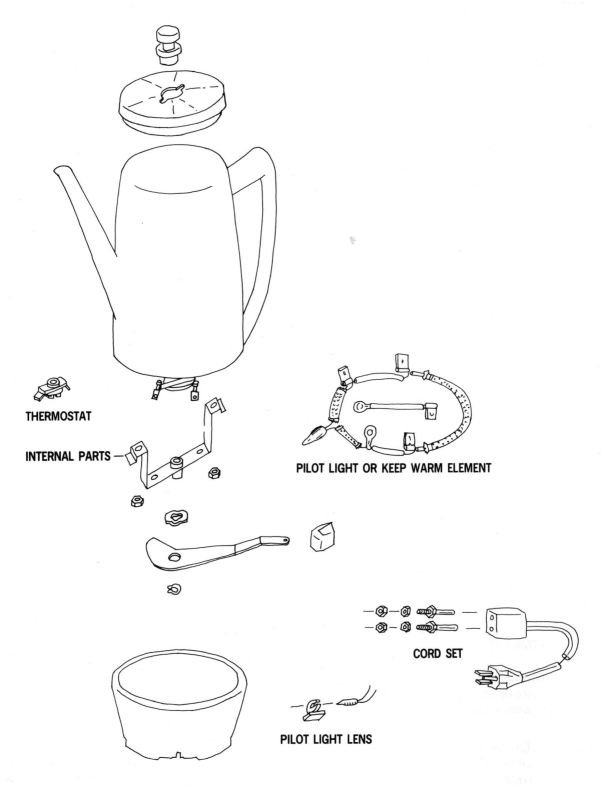

THERMOSTAT

INTERNAL PARTS

PILOT LIGHT OR KEEP WARM ELEMENT

CORD SET

PILOT LIGHT LENS

Fig. 6. Typical coffee maker, alternate model.

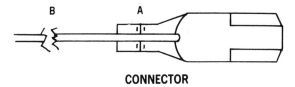

CONNECTOR

Fig. 7. Connector.

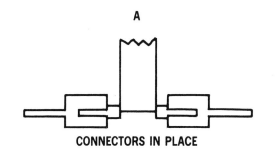

A

CONNECTORS IN PLACE

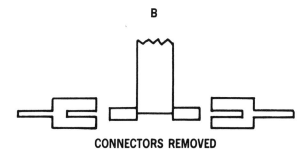

B

CONNECTORS REMOVED

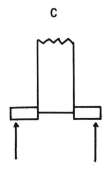

C

ATTACH TEST LIGHT ACROSS HERE

Fig. 8. Thermostat assembly and lead arrangement: (A) connectors in place; (B) connectors removed; (C) attach test light across here.

Step 3—Disassemble the thermostat bracket and remove. The thermostat is usually fastened to the bracket by a small nut. Re-

move the thermostat and replace with a new unit. Bring the old one with you when you go to the supply shop. Reassemble bracket and connect the two wire leads to the thermostat terminals. Reinstall the base. Proceed to Step 4.

Step 4—Fill the coffee maker with cold water and turn it on.

Does the water quickly come to a boil?

Yes—The fault has been isolated and repaired.

No—Proceed to **1040**.

1040

Heating element defective or has failed

If you have found the wiring connections to be tightly made, no broken wires, and the thermostat in working condition you have localized the problem to the heating element. Proceed to Step 1.

Step 1—Disconnect the two leads to the heating element. Check the heater with test light. Connect the alligator clip to one terminal of the heating element and place the probe on the other.

Does the test light light?

Yes—A lighted lamp does not necessarily mean that the heating element is OK, since it is possible that the heater element has burned through but both broken ends are in contact with the metal case.

No—The heater element is defective and must be replaced. Proceed to Step 2.

Step 2—The heater is mounted on the bottom of the coffee pot. The main portion of the element protrudes up into the pot. The pump is inserted onto this protrusion. To remove the heater you must unfasten a large hex nut on the inside of the pot. It is important to use a socket wrench of the correct size in removing this nut. If you don't have one, your local service station will probably be able to assist you. Proceed to Step 3.

Step 3—Carefully remove the heating element, noting the location and position of all the parts, including seals and rings. It is a good idea to make a little sketch so that you can install the heater exactly as you found it. Proceed to Step 4.

Step 4—Obtain an exact replacement of the heater element as well as new washers and rings. Install the new element by retracing the removal procedure. Check that all wire connections are properly replaced and securely fastened. Replace the base and proceed to Step 5.

Step 5—Fill the coffee maker with cold water and turn it on.

Does it quickly come to a boil?

Yes—The fault has been isolated and repaired.

No—If the unit fails to work, remove the base and check to make sure that:
- All connections are firmly made.
- All connectors have been connected to the correct terminals (check disassembly notes).
- No wires were broken during the reassembly process.
- Check continuity of the thermostat and heating elements by using the test light.

The problem must be in one of the above areas.

COFFEE BOILS OR REPERCOLATES

FAULT SYMPTOM 1100

Possible Causes:

- Blockage or defect in pump assembly _____ **See 1110**
- Hot element not kept tight and flush with bottom of base _____ **See 1120**
- "Keeps Hot" element defective _____ **See 1130**
- Thermostat defective _____ **See 1140**

1110

Blockage or defect in pump assembly

Step 1—Remove pump from coffee maker and examine for blockage or defects. Did you find any blockage or defects?

Yes—Clean or replace with new pump. Proceed to Step 2.

No—Proceed to **1120**.

Step 2—Fill the coffee maker with cold water, install pump and basket, and turn on.

Does the water continue to boil or repercolate?

Yes—Proceed to **1120**.

No—The fault has been isolated and corrected.

1120

Hot element not kept tight or flush with bottom of base

Step 1—Place the percolator in an upside down position. Remove the screw or bolt that secures the base assembly to the pot (see Fig. 3) and gently remove the base. On the inside you will see the warming heater. A typical example is shown in Fig. 6. Proceed to Step 2.

Step 2—Check the warming heater to determine if it is securely fastened and flush with the bottom of the base.

Is it tight and flush?

Yes—Proceed to **1130**.

No—Secure the warming heater as required, reassemble, and check the operation of the coffee maker as in **1110,** Step 2.

Does the coffee maker continue to boil or repercolate?

Yes—Proceed to **1130.**

No—The fault has been isolated and corrected.

1130

"Keeps Hot" element defective

Step 1—Remove the base of the percolator as described in Step 1 of **1120.** You will find "Keeps Hot" element in this assembly. A typical example is shown in Fig. 6. Proceed to Step 2.

Step 2—To check the "Keeps Hot" element, connect the alligator clip of a test light to the connector at one end of the "Keeps Hot" element and touch the probe to the other end.

Does the test light light?

Yes—The fault has not been isolated. Proceed to **1140.**

No—The "Keeps Hot" element is defective and must be replaced. Proceed to Step 3.

Step 3—Carefully remove the defective warming element from the base assembly. The leads are generally riveted to the case. To remove them you must grind or file off the rivets. Reassembly must be made with a factory replacement part and rivets. Do not use makeshift parts which can be very dangerous and can result in a fire.

CAUTION

USE ONLY FACTORY AUTHORIZED REPLACEMENT PARTS.

CAUTION

Be sure to make a sketch of locations and connections before disassembly. Proceed to Step 4.

Step 4—Install a new "Keeps Hot" element by retracing the disassembly procedure; use your sketch. Check to be sure all connections are secure and correct. Check the other connections to be sure that nothing was loosened or disconnected during the reassembly. Refasten the base and proceed to Step 5.

Step 5—Fill the coffee maker with cold water, install the pump and basket, and turn on.

Does the coffee maker continue to boil and repercolate?

Yes—Fault not isolated. Proceed to **1140.**

No—Fault isolated and repaired.

1140

Thermostat defective

Step 1—Remove the base of the percolator as described in Step 1 of **1120.** The thermostat location of some typical coffee makers is shown in Fig. 5 and 6. Proceed to Step 2.

Step 2—Remove the connectors from each side of the thermostat; be gentle. See Figs. 4, 5, and 6 for location. Attach the alligator clamp of your test light to one of the terminals on the thermostat and touch the probe to the other terminal, as in Fig. 8A, B, C.

Did the test light glow?

Yes—The thermostat is OK. The fault has not been isolated. You missed a step somewhere. Recheck.

No—The thermostat is defective and must be replaced. Proceed to Step 3.

Step 3—Disassemble the thermostat bracket and remove it. The thermostat is usually fastened to the bracket by a small nut. Remove the thermostat and replace it with a new unit. Take the old one with you to the supply shop. Be sure to make a diagram of locations and connections. Reassemble the bracket and connect the two wires to the thermostat terminals. Follow your diagram. Proceed to Step 4.

Step 4—Fill the coffee maker with cold water, install the pump and basket, and plug in the cord.

Does the water boil or percolate continuously?

Yes—The fault has not been isolated. You missed a step somewhere. Recheck the steps in **1100**.

No—The fault is isolated and corrected.

COFFEE IS WEAK

FAULT SYMPTOM 1200

Possible Causes:

- The heater well is fouled ———————————— **See 1210**
- Thermostat adjustment is incorrect ——————— **See 1220**

Initial Conditions Check List:

Fill the coffee maker to the desired level with *cold* water and make a pot of coffee. Did the coffee taste strong enough?

Yes—Fault isolated. The possible use of warm or hot water reduces the percolating time and can result in weak coffee.

No—Fault verified. Proceed to **1210**.

1210

The heater well is fouled

Step 1—Inspect the inside of the heater well for coffee grounds or deposits.

Are there coffee grounds or deposits?

Yes—Clean out grounds and clean surface with a coffee stain cleaner. Proceed to Step 2.

No—Fault not isolated. Proceed to **1220**.

Step 2—Fill the coffee maker to the desired level with cold water and

brew a pot of coffee.
Did the coffee taste strong enough?

Yes—Fault isolated and corrected.

No—Proceed to **1220**.

1220

Thermostat adjustment is incorrect

Some coffee makers feature a thermostat adjustment screw. It is located below the logo name plate on the base of the percolator. Lift the upper right corner of the name plate and rotate it counter clockwise. Withdraw the access screw and gasket to expose the slotted adjusting screw. Turning the adjusting screw (use a small bladed screwdriver) *clockwise* decreases the water temperature; turning it *counterclockwise* increases the temperature. The temperature of the water for proper brewing should be between 181°F and 195°F. Proceed to Step 1.

Step 1—Fill the coffee maker with cold water and start it. Insert a thermometer (a candy thermometer will do) in the water. When it stops rising take a reading.

Is the temperature below 181°F?

Yes—The cause of your weak coffee may have been isolated. Proceed to Step 2.

No—Proceed to Step 2.

Step 2—Turn the adjusting screw counterclockwise 1/8th of a turn. Check the temperature on the thermometer. Continue to make small adjustments until your thermometer reaches 181° but not more than 195°.

Were you able to adjust the temperature?

Yes—The fault has been isolated and corrected.

No—The heating element may be defective. Refer to **1040**.

COFFEE IS BITTER

FAULT SYMPTOM 1300

Possible Causes:

- Interior of percolator, basket, pump is stained or covered with a residue.

  Inspect and clean with a cleaner intended for coffee makers, such as "Dip It."

COFFEE DOES NOT STAY WARM AFTER BREWING

FAULT SYMPTOM 1400

Possible Causes:

- Thermostat is defective _____ **See 1410**
- "Keeps Hot" element is defective _____ **See 1420**

1410

Thermostat is defective

Refer to **1030** for step-by-step procedures.

1420

"Keeps Hot" element is defective

Refer to **1040** for step-by-step procedures.

CORN POPPERS

UNIT WILL NOT HEAT

FAULT SYMPTOM 2000

Possible Causes:

- Power cord defective _____ **See 2010**
- Internal wire assembly defective _____ **See 2020**
- Thermostat is defective _____ **See 2030**
- Heating element defective _____ **See 2040**

Initial Conditions Check List:

a. Plug a table lamp in the power receptacle to be sure you have a live circuit.

b. Turn the popper switch, if there is one, to the START position.

c. Check to be sure the proper type of corn is being used. It must be clearly marked "For Popping" or "For Pop Corn."

Perform the above and turn the popper on carefully. Does the popper heat continuously?

Yes—The fault is not verified. One of the initial conditions must have been overlooked.

No—Proceed to **2010**.

2010

Power cord defective

Step 1—Unplug the cord. Remove the cord set from the popper. Ex-amine the cord set to make sure it has not had extensive wear or that the appliance plug is not corroded from arcing. Look for breaks in the insulation and fraying where the wires enter the receptacle and appliance plug. Check the inside of the appliance plug for pitting and dark burn marks (see Fig. 1).

Is the cord set in good condition?

Yes—Proceed to Step 3.

No—Replace the cord set and proceed to Step 2.

Step 2—Follow the instructions for popping in your user manual and pop a batch.

Did the corn pop properly?

Yes—The fault has been isolated and corrected.

No—There are additional faults that can

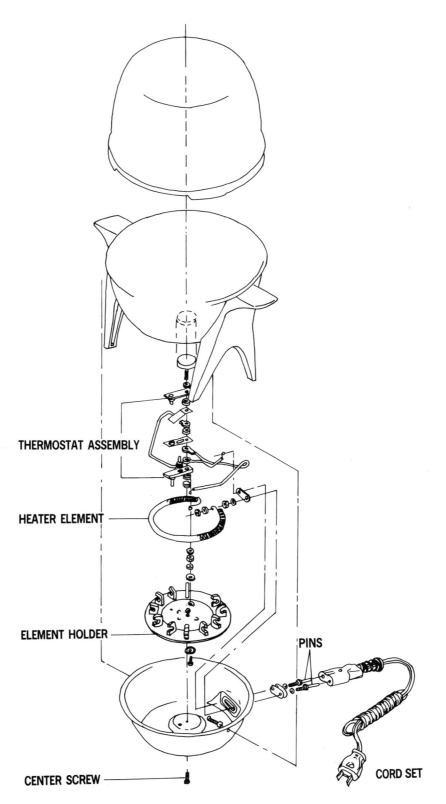

THERMOSTAT ASSEMBLY

HEATER ELEMENT

ELEMENT HOLDER

PINS

CORD SET

CENTER SCREW

Fig. 9. Typical corn popper base.

be checked and corrected. Proceed to **2020**.

Step **3**—Check the cord set for poor connections or breaks in the wire with a test light. Refer to Service Procedure **11000**.

Does the cord set check out OK?

Yes—Fault has not been isolated. Proceed to **2020**.

No—Replace the cord set and follow Step 2.

2020

Internal wire assembly defective

CAUTION

BE SURE THE POPPER IS DISCONNECTED FROM THE POWER RECEPTACLE.

CAUTION

Step **1**—Remove the cover or any other loose elements of the popper. Turn the popper upside down. On most units you will find two screws on the bottom, as shown in Fig. 9.
When you remove these screws you should be able to remove the base assembly from the bowl. Do this very gently.

NOTE:

On some poppers there are three screws. Remove only the two outside screws. The center screw holds the internal assembly to the base.

You will have now exposed the heater element disc, the thermostat, the wiring assembly, and associated fasteners. See Fig. 10.

Step **2**—Inspect the terminal pins. Make sure they are securely fas-

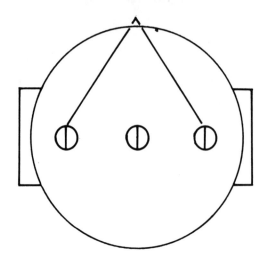

REMOVE THESE SCREWS

DO NOT REMOVE CENTER SCREW

Fig. 10. Typical popper internal assembly.

tened. Check that the inside leads are all securely connected and there are no breaks in the wires.

Did you find the wiring and connections OK?

Yes—Proceed to Step 4.

No—Proceed to Step 3.

Fig. 11. Slip-on connector.

Step **3**—If a wire lead is to be replaced, examine each end at its connection point. If the connection is a slip-on, as shown in Fig. 11, gently work the connector free at each end and replace it with a factory replacement. If the connector is soldered, heat the soldered joint with a soldering gun while gently pulling the wire with needle-nosed pliers. When the solder melts, the wire will pull free. Replace with a new wire of the same type. Proceed to Step 4.

NOTE:

If solder does not melt, the connection has been made up with silver solder. To separate this connection you must use a high temperature torch. Select a fine tip for the torch and mask the area around the connection to be heated with a piece of asbestos or several layers of fiber glass. Replace the broken lead with a new wire of the same type. Resolder following the steps of the removal procedure. Proceed to Step 4.

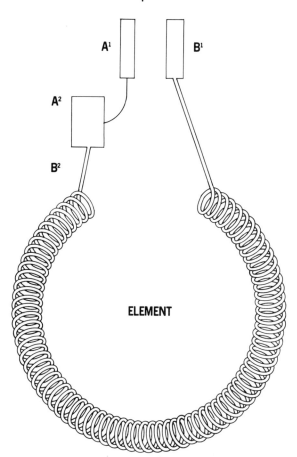

Fig. 12. Typical popper heater element.

Step 4—Using a probe test light, attach the alligator clamp to one outside terminal pin (A¹) and check the continuity to the thermostat connection (A¹ to A²), as shown in Fig. 12. If the

probe light glows, the circuit is OK. Now check between B¹ and B².

Did the lamp glow in both tests?

Yes—The connecting circuits are OK. Reassemble and proceed to Step 5.

No—Recheck the wiring as described in Steps 1 and 2. You may have overlooked something.

Step 5—Plug in the corn popper and pop a batch of corn.

Did it pop satisfactorily?

Yes—Fault isolated and corrected.

No—Proceed to **2030**.

2030

Thermostat is defective

Step 1—The thermostat in the popper controls the heat and prevents the popper from overheating. If the popper has had very heavy and continuous use then the thermostat may not fully close after the popper cools. Thus the next time the popper is used it won't heat. If the contact points of the thermostat are not in an enclosed unit (see Fig. 12), check them for arcing. Refer to **2020** for disassembly. If they are blue or black and obvious evidence of burning/black carbon is present, the thermostat must be replaced. Proceed to Step 2.

Step 2—Use a test light and check the thermostat for continuity. Refer to **2020**, Step 3. The test light should glow if the circuit is OK. Before doing the test, gently remove the connectors from each side of the thermostat (see Fig. 10 as reference). Attach the alligator clamp of the test light to one of the thermostat terminals and touch the probe to the other terminal.

Did the light glow; is the contact in good condition?

Yes—The thermostat is not the cause of the problem. Proceed to **2040**.

No—The thermostat needs to be replaced. Proceed to Step 3.

Step 3—Disassemble the thermostat. Make a wire connection sketch as you disassemble it so that you can replace all the parts exactly. Obtain a new exact replacement part from an authorized distributor. Install the new thermostat. Make sure all connections are firm. Proceed to Step 4.

Step 4—Completely reassemble the proper. Plug in the unit and pop some corn.

Did the popper perform satisfactorily?

Yes—The fault has been isolated and corrected.

No—Proceed to **2040**.

2040

Heating element defective

Step 1—Most heater elements consist of nichrome wire wound like a spring and assembled on an element disc by porcelain mounts. Refer to **2020** to disassemble units. Inspect the wire heating element for breaks or thin spots.

Are there broken mounts or does the heating element look suspect?

Yes—The heating element or supports must be replaced. Proceed to Step 2.

No—You overlooked something in **2010**, **2020**, or **2030**. Recheck.

Step 2—Remove the screw or hex nut fastener that holds the heater element disc assembly to the base. Be sure to make a sketch. Loosen and remove the two wire leads attached to the external terminal pins and remove the assembly (see Fig. 10). Inspect and replace any porcelain supports that are broken or damaged. Carefully install an exact factory replacement heater element. Retrace all the steps you recorded on your sketch. Be careful not to stretch or damage the nichrome wire during installation. Check all leads to be sure they are securely fastened and that nothing was damaged or displaced during the installation of the heater element. Proceed to Step 3.

Step 3—Reassemble the popper. Make sure that the thermostat seats firmly against the bottom of the popper bowl. Proceed to Step 4.

Step 4—Pop some corn to check out the popper.

Does the corn pop OK?

Yes—Problem isolated and corrected.

No—You overlooked something. Review the procedures of **2000**.

POPPER OVERHEATS; BURNS CORN; WILL NOT SHUT OFF
FAULT SYMPTOM 2100

Possible Cause:

- Thermostat is defective
  Refer to **2030** for step-by-step procedure.

CORN WILL NOT POP

FAULT SYMPTOM 2200

Possible Causes:

- Thermostat defective _____ **See 2210**
- Heating element defective _____ **See 2220**

2210

2220

Thermostat defective

Refer to **2030** for step-by-step procedure.

Heating element defective

Refer to **2040** for step-by-step procedure.

FRY PANS

UNIT WILL NOT HEAT

Possible Causes:

* Cord set defective ———————————— **See 3010**
* Thermostat defective ———————————— **See 3020**
* Heating element defective ——————— **See 3030**

Many fry pans are immersible in water. This means that the control unit must be separate and detachable from the appliance. The fry pan consists, therefore, of three main assemblies. See Fig. 13. The pan assembly is manufactured with a cal-rod heating element cast into the pan so that it is not removable and replaceable. This unit is very unlikely to fail. If the fry pan does not heat, the problem is likely to be the thermostat or the cord set and not the heating element.

Initial Conditions Check List:

a. Plug a table lamp into the kitchen power receptacle to be sure you have a live outlet.
b. Check to see that the switch is ON.

Step 1—Fill the fry pan half full with water. Set the control knob at full ON (420°F).

Does the water come to a boil?

Yes—Fault not verified. You must have overlooked an initial condition.

No—Fault verified. Proceed to **3010.**

3010

Cord set defective

Step 1—Examine the cord set for wear. Look for breaks in the insulation and for fraying where the wires enter the receptacle and appliance plug. Check the inside of the appliance plug for pitting and dark brown marks. This is caused by removing the appliance end of the cord before removing the wall receptacle end.

Is the cord set in good condition?

Yes—Proceed to Step 3.

No—Replace the cord set with a factory replacement part. Proceed to Step 2.

Step 2—Most cord set control units can be disassembled by removing two or three screws. Carefully undo the connections in the

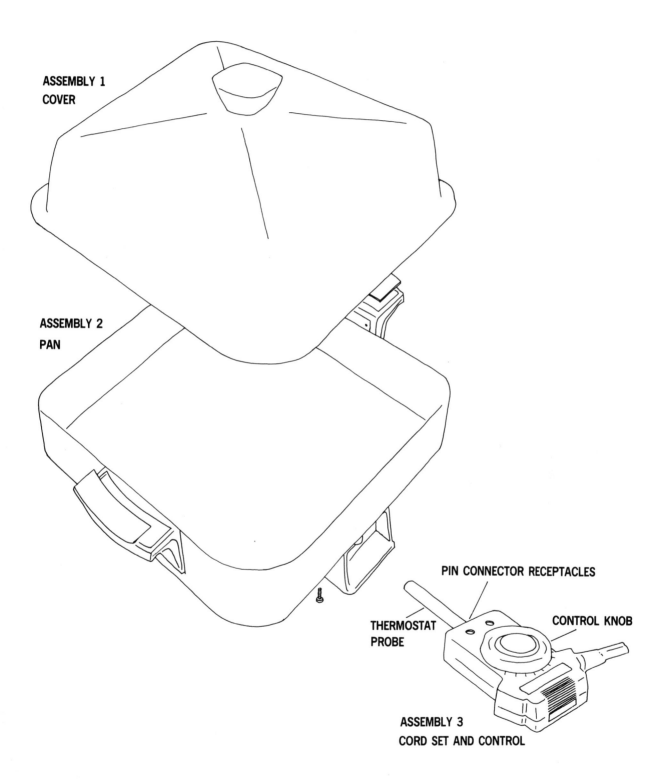

ASSEMBLY 1
COVER

ASSEMBLY 2
PAN

PIN CONNECTOR RECEPTACLES

THERMOSTAT
PROBE

CONTROL KNOB

ASSEMBLY 3
CORD SET AND CONTROL

Fig. 13. Typical fry pan.

control unit and install a factory replacement cord set. Be careful not to dislodge any of the parts in the control unit. Make sure the connections are secure. If only the wall receptacle end seems to be in poor repair, cut this end off and replace with a new receptacle. If the recessed pin connectors in the control unit are pitted, these may be cleaned by forming a piece of sandpaper into a cylinder or roll. Insert and rotate this sandpaper cylinder in the receptacle holes. If the pitting is extensive, cleaning will not provide a long-lasting repair, and replacement of the control is required. Reassemble the control unit and proceed to Step 3.

Step 3—Fill the pan half full with water. Set the control knob at full ON.

Does the water come to a boil?

Yes—Fault has been isolated and repaired.

No—Proceed to **3020**.

3020

Thermostat defective

Step 1—Detach and/or unplug the cord set from the fry pan. Use a probe light tester and attach the alligator clamp of the tester to one of the terminals on the plug end of the wire cord set. Insert the other probe in the recessed pin receptacle, as shown in Fig. 14. Be sure the control knob is turned ON. If the probe light does not glow, insert the probe into the other pin receptacle. Next, try the other terminal and pin receptacle pair. Turn the control knob to OFF and ON as you perform this test. The probe light should glow when the control is ON throughout its range and go out when turned OFF. If the light goes off during this test, there is a problem in the thermostat or variable control. If the test light does not glow at all, the thermostat is defective and probably stuck in the open position. In either event it will be necessary to replace the entire control unit. Do not throw the unit away; it generally has a trade-in value when purchasing a factory replacement unit. Proceed to Step 2.

Step 2—Using the new or replacment control unit, test the fry pan as in Step 3 of **3020**.

Does the water come to a boil?

CONTROL

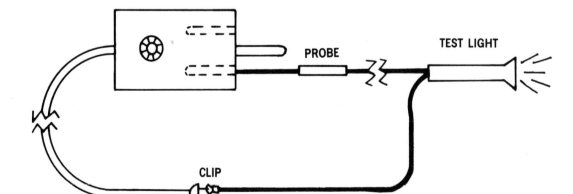

Fig. 14. Test light set up.

Yes—Fault has been isolated and repaired.

No—Review the steps in **3000** to determine if you overlooked something. If not, go to **3030**.

3030

Heating element defective

CAUTION

BE SURE PAN IS UNPLUGGED AND COOL.

CAUTION

Step 1—To check the fry pan heating element insert test light alligator clip into one of the fry pan receptacle pins. Place the test light probe in the other. Turn ON.

Does the light glow?

Yes—The heating element is OK. Refer again to **3000**.

No—The heating element is defective. The fry pan is not repairable and should be discarded.

2037717

PAN DOES NOT GET HOT ENOUGH

FAULT SYMPTOM 3100

Possible Causes:
- Control knob loose _____ **See 3110**
- Thermostat defective _____ **See 3120**

3110

Control knob loose

Check the control knob and try to determine if it is rotating the shaft without slipping.

Is it firmly attached to the shaft? Does it feel as though it is slipping or loose?

Yes—Proceed to **3120**.

No—Take the control to a parts dealer and see if a replacement knob can be obtained.

3120

Thermostat defective

Fill the fry pan half full with water. Set the control knob at full ON (about 420°F). Wait for the water to come to a boil.

Does the water boil?

Yes—Fault not verified.

No—Fault is verified. The thermostat in the control is defective. The entire control unit must be replaced. The age and condition of the fry pan should be taken into account to justify replacement of this part.

PAN OVERHEATS

Possible Causes:

- Control shaft is stuck in the full ON position _____ **See 3210**
- The thermostat is defective _____ **See 3220**

3210

Control shaft stuck in full ON position

Check the control knob to see if it is rotating the shaft as it is moved from OFF to ON.

Can you turn the fry pan on and off?

Yes—Fault does not seem to be associated with control knob. Proceed to **3220**.

No—Control shaft must be replaced. Check with a parts dealer for a new shaft. If unavailable, replace control unit.

3220

Thermostat is defective

Step 1—Fill the fry pan half full with water. Set the control knob at full ON (420°). Wait five minutes after water comes to a boil. Turn the control knob down until the light goes out. Proceed to Step 2.

Step 2—With a candy thermometer, check the temperature when the light goes out. If the temperature is between 180°–220°F the control is satisfactory.

Is the temperature between 180°–220°F?

Yes—The fry pan is operating as it should. You may have had the control in full ON.

No—The control is defective and needs to be replaced.

GRIDDLES and GRILLS

UNIT WILL NOT HEAT

FAULT SYMPTOM 4000

Possible Causes:

- Power cord defective _____ **See 4010**
- Internal wire connections loose or broken _____ **See 4020**
- Thermostat defective _____ **See 4030**
- Heating element defective _____ **See 4040**

Initial Conditions Check List:

a. Plug a table lamp into the electric service outlet to be sure you have a live outlet.
b. If the unit has an On-Off switch, put it in the ON position.
c. Be sure to use or mix the proper dough mixture. Follow the mix package or cookbook directions carefully.

Plug the unit into the outlet and turn it on. Do this several times.

Does the unit heat each time?

Yes—Fault not verified. An initial condition must have been overlooked.

No—Proceed to **4010.**

4010

Power cord defective

CAUTION

UNPLUG APPLIANCE.

CAUTION

Step 1—Examine the cord set to make sure it has not had extensive wear or that the appliance plug is not corroded from arcing. Look for breaks in the insulation and fraying where the wires enter the receptacle and appliance plug. Check the inside of the appliance plug for pitting and dark burn marks (see Fig. 1).

Is the cord set in good condition?

Yes—Proceed to Step 3.

No—Replace the cord set and proceed to Step 2.

Step 2—Plug the unit into an active outlet and turn on.

Does it heat?

Yes—Fault isolated and corrected.

No—Proceed to **4020.**

Most grills are dual purpose appliances. They can be used as a grill, and, by reversing the grill surface, they become a waffle maker. On units such as these, when the grid is removed the wiring assembly is exposed and can be tested.

CAUTION

BE SURE TO UNPLUG UNIT FROM THE POWER SOURCE SERVICE OUTLET.

CAUTION

Step 3—Remove the two grid assemblies and trace the wires entering the base to the place where they are connected to the internal assembly, usually a heavy riveted mechanical connection, as shown in Fig. 15. Proceed to Step 4.

NOTE:

Be sure to check both plug prongs for each one of the riveted connections.

Yes—The connecting cord is OK. Proceed to **4020.**

No—The cord must be replaced. Proceed to Step 5.

Step 5—Cut the two cord set wire leads inside the grill. Remove the cord through the opening in the grill at the point where there is a grommet. Check for a metal retaining clip fastened on the cord inside the grill. Remove this clip before attempting to remove the cord. The clip can be removed by simply clipping the wire at the base. Insert a new wire of the same type through the grommet. Be sure to strip—remove the insulation from the wire ends—before inserting into grill. If the wires were fastened by a screw connector, refasten in the same manner. If a mechanical clip was used, then fasten with this clip. If the wire lead connection was a solder connection, heat the connection with your soldering gun or

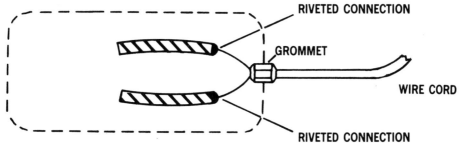

RIVETED CONNECTION

GROMMET

WIRE CORD

RIVETED CONNECTION

Fig. 15. Typical grill assembly.

Step 4—Adjust the control lever to the OFF position and check continuity between the riveted connections and the cord set plug prongs. See Test Procedure **11000** for continuity check procedure.

Does the test lamp light for both leads?

torch until the solder softens. Remove the old piece of wire remaining by gently pulling on it while heating, and discard it. Attach the new lead. Be sure you have a secure connection. Replace the wire retaining clip on the inside, reassemble the grill, and proceed to Step 6.

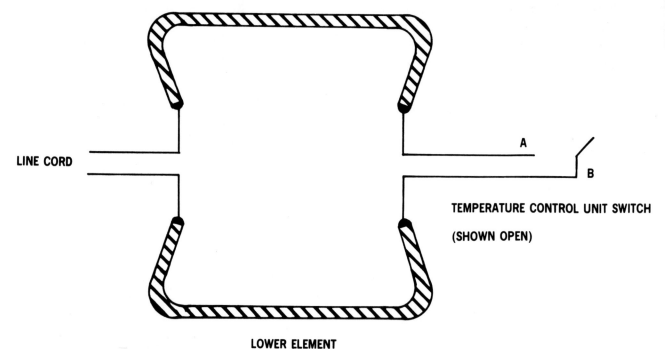

UPPER HEATING ELEMENT

LINE CORD

A

B

TEMPERATURE CONTROL UNIT SWITCH

(SHOWN OPEN)

LOWER ELEMENT

Fig. 16. Typical grill elements.

Step 6—Plug the cord into a live outlet. Turn the unit on.

Does it heat?

Yes—The fault has been isolated and corrected.

No—Proceed to **4020**.

4020

Internal wire connections loose or broken

Step 1—Normally the internal wire assembly consists only of two heavy wires that run from the cord to the heater element. Unplug the unit and examine these first to make sure they are not broken. Move them gently to make sure they are firmly connected to the incoming leads and heater elements. Use a test probe to check continuity either between the connection at the lead and the heater element, or between the wall plug of the cord and the heater element. If the probe light does not glow, the connection or the cord is defective.

Does the test probe light glow?

Yes—The fault has not been isolated. Proceed to **4030**.

No—The fault has been located. Replace the cord or repair the connections as noted in **4010**. Proceed to Step 2.

NOTE 1:

If these leads are fastened to the heating element by a soldered connection, replacement must be completed by the use of silver solder and a propane torch. Lead or tin solder is not used because the heat from the element would melt the tin solder.

NOTE 2:

These leads are asbestos wrapped to protect them from the high heat within the grill. Exact replacement wires should be obtained from an authorized parts supplier.

Step 2—Plug the cord into a live circuit; turn the unit on.

Does it heat?

Yes—The fault has been isolated and corrected.

No—Proceed to **4030**.

4030

Thermostat defective

Most grills have a temperature control device to sense the heat and turn the heating elements on and off. This component is arranged as shown in Fig. 16.

The temperature control unit switch is shown open in the sketch. It is normally closed. When closed, this allows the grill to start heating as soon as it is plugged in and the control turned to ON. When the unit reaches the maximum temperature, the control opens until a predetermined lower level is reached. Then the switch closes and again turns on the current.

Step 1—Unplug the griddle. Turn the control knob to OFF. Test for continuity across the terminals of the control unit with a test probe (A and B in Fig. 16).

Does the light in the test probe glow?

NOTE:

The test light should glow through the full range of control knob adjustment except OFF.

Yes—Temperature control unit is defective. Proceed to Step 2.

No—The temperature control unit is OK. Proceed to **4040**.

CAUTION

BE CERTAIN THE UNIT HAS BEEN UNPLUGGED FROM ELECTRICAL OUTLET.

CAUTION

Step 2—Replace the temperature control unit with a factory replacement part. Take the defective part with you to your supplier. Proceed to Step 3.

Step 3—Disconnect the leads that are attached to the temperature control (there are two). Mark the leads as they are removed so that the leads of the replacement unit will be returned to the same connections on reassembly. Remove the element support plate (see figure in **4010**).

NOTE 1:

It may be necessary to loosen and remove the element support plate in order to reach the terminals on the temperature control unit and finally reach and disconnect the leads. Be careful not to move the element supports too much or they may break or damage the wires.

NOTE 2:

Examine the control and observe how it is fastened to the base of the grill. If the unit is attached with rivets, you will have to drill out the rivets and later reassemble using small bolts, lock washers, and nuts. Proceed to Step 4.

Step 4—Install the new unit following the reverse order of removal. *Be sure* that wires are firmly connected and installed on supports or anchor points and that no bare wires are in contact with the metal base of the grill. Proceed to Step 5.

CAUTION

CHECK YOUR WORK. BARE WIRES MUST NOT BE IN CONTACT WITH METAL PARTS OF THE GRILL.

CAUTION

Step 5—After reassembly of the control, install the grill plate, reassemble grill, and test the grill by operating through a complete cycle. Use caution and plug grill in with only one hand.

Does the grill operate normally?

Yes—Fault has been isolated and repaired.

No—Proceed to **4040**.

4040

Heating element defective

The heating elements are usually made of nichrome wire coiled to look like a spring. The elements are attached to the upper and lower element supports by porcelain insulators which extend ½ to 1 inch from the base of the supports. After prolonged use the elements may become brittle and break if the grill is dropped or set down hard.

Step 1—Unplug the grill. Remove the grid and expose the heating unit. Examine the upper and lower units; move them gently to make sure they are not broken. Also look for areas or points where pitting or burning appears to have occurred.

Are the elements broken, burned, or pitted?

Yes—The heating element is defective and must be replaced. Proceed to Step 3.

No—The fault has not been isolated. Proceed to Step 2.

Step 2—With a test probe check the continuity of each element at the point where they connect to the internal wiring (see figures in **4010** and **4030**).

Does the test light glow?

Yes—The heating elements are OK. You must have overlooked a procedure. Recheck the steps in **4000**.

No—The elements are defective. Proceed to Step 3.

NOTE:

Even if only one element has failed it is recommended that both be replaced. Be sure to use an exact factory replacement part.

Step 3—To replace the heating elements, remove the end of the element that attaches to the input power line and the end that attaches to the temperature control.

NOTE:

If the inside of your grill has become coated with a layer of grease, this must be cleaned before reassembly. If you use a cleaning fluid for this purpose, be sure that it has all evaporated before you turn on the unit.

CAUTION

DO NOT TURN ON UNIT IN THE PRESENCE OF CLEANING FLUIDS.

CAUTION

UNIT DOES NOT FULLY HEAT WITH CONTROL AT HIGH SETTING   FAULT SYMPTOM 4100

Possible Causes:

- "Tired" heating element ————————————— See 4110
- Defective control unit ————————————— See 4120

4110

"Tired" heating element

Step 1— Unplug the line cord. Open the grill and remove the upper and lower grid plates. The heating elements are now visible. Proceed to Step 2.

CAUTION

THE NEXT STEP INVOLVES A LIVE ELECTRICAL TEST. USE GREAT CAUTION. FOR SAFETY, USE ONE HAND ONLY; PLACE OTHER HAND IN POCKET. DO NOT TOUCH GRILL WITH OTHER HAND. DO NOT CONDUCT THIS TEST NEAR WATER OR A SINK.

CAUTION

Step 2—Plug the line cord into a live house outlet. Set the control to the highest setting. Wait for the unit to heat. Proceed to Step 3.

CAUTION

DO NOT TOUCH THE INSIDE OF THE UNIT WITH FINGERS OR TOOLS.

CAUTION

Step 3—When the unit has reached maximum temperature, the heating elements should be cherry red, with no dark spots or dark areas.

Do the elements glow cherry red without dark areas?

Yes—The fault has not been found. Proceed to Step 4.

No—Unplug the grill. The fault probably lies in the heater control. Refer to **4120**.

Step 4—*Visually* examine the elements for dark spots or dark areas.

Try to determine if the heating element is orange rather than bright red.

Did you find dark or dull areas or that the element is only orange color not bright cherry red?

Yes—The heating element is defective. Unplug the grill. Replace the element with a factory replacement part. Refer to **4040**.

No—The fault has not been verified. Unplug the grill. Check the previous steps. You may have overlooked an operating procedure. Reassemble the grill.

4120

Defective control unit

Refer to **4030** for step-by-step procedure.

CLOTHES IRONS, DRY

IRON WILL NOT HEAT

FAULT SYMPTOM 5000

Possible Causes:

- Defective cord set _____ **See 5010**
- Defective thermostat _____ **See 5020**
- Heating element has failed _____ **See 5030**

In most electric clothes pressing irons the electric heating element is an integral part of the sole plate (the bottom plate). Therefore, this part is not replaceable. The heating element, however, is a very reliable, long lasting part of the iron and does not usually fail. Figure 17 is an example of a typical standard dry iron heating element and temperature control unit.

Initial Conditions Check List:

a. Plug a table lamp in the wall electric outlet to be sure you have a live circuit.
b. Set the iron control knob at the desired temperature. Does the iron heat? Repeat a number of times. Allow iron to cool between tests.

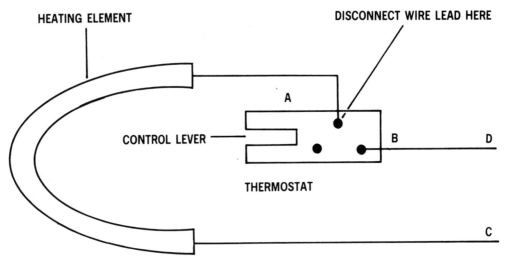

Fig. 17. Heating elements and temperature control unit.

Yes—Fault not verified. You must have overlooked an initial condition.

No—Fault verified. Proceed to **5010**.

5010

Defective cord set

Step 1—Unplug the cord from outlet. Examine the cord for breaks, especially at the plug end.

Is the cord OK?

Yes—Proceed to Step 3.

No—The cord must be replaced. Proceed to Step 2.

Step 2—Turn the iron upside down and look at the heel and locate the rating plate.

CAUTION

DO NOT PROCEED BEFORE REMOVING THE CORD FROM THE WALL OUTLET.

CAUTION

This plate is usually fastened in place with a small screw. On some irons, this plate is a snap-on and must be pried out. On other irons, there is a plastic cover at the rear of the handle that is secured in place with one or two small screws. Remove the plate or cover. You will now have access to the connection terminals of the cord set. Proceed to Step 3.

Step 3—Turn the temperature control to OFF. Connect the alligator clamp of a test probe lamp (see Service Procedure **11000**) to one prong of the cord plug and

touch the two inside connections (one at a time) with the tip of the other probe. At one of these connections the test lamp should glow. Move the cord set and manipulate the plug to make sure the test light continues to glow. Move the alligator clamp to the other prong of the plug and touch the connection point which did not cause the test lamp to glow during this test.

Did the test light glow in both cases?

Yes—The cord set is OK. Proceed to **5020**.

No—The cord is defective. Proceed to Step 4.

NOTE:

When the alligator clamp is attached to one prong of the plug and BOTH terminal connections in the iron cause the test light to glow, then check the control switch. It should be in the OFF position. If it is OFF and both connections cause the light to glow, there is a problem in the thermostat. Proceed to **5020**.

Step 4—Obtain and install a factory replacement cord. Replace the plate or cover, and proceed to Step 5.

Step 5—Plug the iron into a live wall circuit. Turn the control to one of the temperature settings.

Does the iron heat up?

Yes—The fault had been isolated and corrected.

No—Proceed to **5020**.

5020

Defective thermostat

CAUTION

UNPLUG THE IRON FROM THE POWER SOURCE.

CAUTION

Step 1—To get at the thermostat, you will have to remove the handle. Each iron is designed slightly differently from others, but handle removal is usually not difficult. On most models this is done by prying up the name plate with a screwdriver. There are two screws which secure the handle to the iron. Remove these screws. Also disconnect the two screws which attach the power cord to the iron. Some irons have long screws which go through the upright portion of the handle. On others, the screws must be reached through a removable part of the handle. With the handle removed, you will find a screw which holds the top of the iron to the sole. Remove this screw and carefully lift the top off. Sometimes it will be necessary to insert a sharp blade along the sole to loosen the top. Proceed to Step 2.

Step 2—Examine the control to be sure the shaft rotates when the control knob is adjusted.

Does the control shaft rotate?

Yes—Proceed to Step 3.

No—Replace the control with an exact factory replacement part. Reassemble iron and repeat initial condition test.

Step 3—Inspect the thermostat (see Fig. 17) for pitting of the contact points or evidence of the points welded together. Examine the springs to make sure they are under tension and not broken.

Are the contacts and springs OK?

Yes—Proceed to Step 4.

No—The thermostat must be replaced. Proceed to Step 4.

Step 4—Disconnect the lead that comes from the heating element to the thermostat, refer to Fig. 17. Use a test probe light (see Service Procedure **11000**) to check the continuity between "A" and "B" with the lead to "A" disconnected. Move the control lever with your finger. The test lamp should go off and on as the thermostat points open and close.

Does the test light go on and off?

Yes—Proceed to Step 5.

No—The thermostat is defective. Proceed to Step 6.

NOTE:

Before replacing the thermostat you should check to see if the heating element is operative. It is most unlikely that the element is bad, but it would be a waste to replace a thermostat and then find the iron had a defective heating element and could not be repaired. Refer to **5030** to check the heating element.

Step 5—Reconnect the lead to terminal "A" and check the continuity between points "C" and "D" with your test light. Open and close the points of the thermostat. The test light should glow when the points are closed.

Does the test light glow when the contact points are closed?

Yes—Proceed to **5030**.

No—The thermostat is defective. Proceed to Step 6.

Step 6—The thermostat usually is secured to the sole of the iron by two or more screws. Hold the iron securely and remove the retaining screws. The thermostat can then be easily removed. Proceed to Step 7.

Step 7—Obtain an exact factory replacement thermostat (take the old part with you) and install in the reverse order of disassembly. *All screws must be securely tightened.* Reconnect the lead from the heating element to the correct terminal of the thermostat. Proceed to Step 8.

NOTE:

Should the short wire lead that runs from the thermostat to the cord set not come as part of the thermostat assembly, the lead must also be replaced. This lead must either be brazed or silver soldered to the thermostat. Brazing must be done at a welding shop. Silver soldering may be done at home with a high-temperature torch equipped with a fine blade tip. Check with your parts supplier to determine the correct way of making this connection.

Step 8—Replace the top, making sure that the temperature shaft assembly is correctly aligned with the control lever of the thermo-

stat. Replace the rating plate or the back of the handle as applicable. Proceed to Step 9.

Step 9—Plug the iron into the house electrical outlet and set the thermostat at some desired range. Do this for a number of different settings, allowing the iron to cool between tests.

Does the iron operate normally ?

Yes—The fault has been isolated and repaired.

No—Proceed to **5030**.

5030

Heating element has failed

Step 1—Refer to Fig. 17. Use a test light (Service Procedure **11000**) to check continuity between "A" and "C". Lead at "A" should be disconnected from its terminal. If the test light glows, the heating element is satisfactory.

Does the test light glow?

Yes—Heating element is OK.

No—The element is defective and the iron cannot be repaired.

CLOTHES IRONS, STEAM

The steam iron works on the same general principle as the dry iron. It has a heating element in the sole, a thermostat to control the temperature and the same wiring system.

The difference is that the steam iron also contains a water reservoir tank and valves to control the water flow. See Fig. 18 for an example of a dissassembled steam iron. When steam is desired, the release knob in the handle at 'A' is pressed. This allows water to run into the cavity ('B') in the sole of the iron ('C') where the water is turned into steam. The steam escapes through the holes on the bottom of the iron.

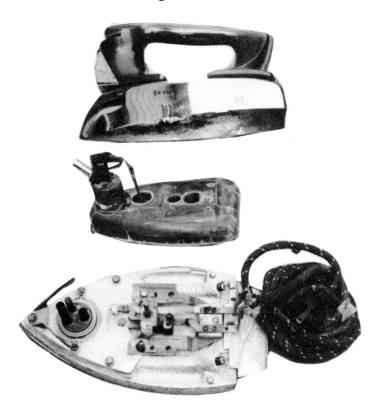

Fig. 18. Typical steam iron, disassembled.

IRON WILL NOT HEAT

FAULT SYMPTOM 6000

Possible Causes:

- Defective cord set _____ **See 5010**
- Defective thermostat _____ **See 5020**
- Heating element has failed _____ **See 5030**

IRON HEAT CANNOT BE ADJUSTED

FAULT SYMPTOM 6100

Possible Causes:

- Control knob is loose _____ **See 6110**
- Thermostat is defective _____ **See 6120**

6110

Control knob is loose

Refer to **5020** to get at the control knob connection. Rotate the control knob and observe if the knob engages the shaft causing it to turn.

Does the knob properly engage the shaft?

Yes—Proceed to **5120**.

No—Refer to **5020**, Steps 1 and 2, for inspection of shaft and thermostat control.

6120

Thermostat is defective

Refer to **5020** for testing and replacement of a defective thermostat.

IRON LEAKS

FAULT SYMPTOM 6200

Possible Causes:

- Steam chamber leaks ⎯⎯⎯⎯⎯⎯⎯⎯⎯⎯**See 6210**
- Water release valve defective ⎯⎯⎯⎯⎯⎯**See 6220**
- Reservoir leaks ⎯⎯⎯⎯⎯⎯⎯⎯⎯⎯⎯⎯**See 6230**

Initial Conditions Check List:

What appears to be a leak may be the result of overfilling the reservoir. Check the manufacturer's instructions. Has the iron been overfilled?

Yes—Proceed to Step 1.

No—Proceed to **6210**.

Step 1—Fill the reservoir to the correct level, plug in the iron and operate.

Does the iron leak?

Yes—The fault has been verified. Proceed to **6210**.

No—The fault was not verified. The iron was overfilled. If the iron has been operated as a dry iron for an extended period, there may be what appears to be a leak when none exists. Has the iron been operated dry for a long period?

Yes— Proceed to Step 2.

No—Proceed to **6210**.

Step 2—Fill the iron with water and operate with the control at the highest setting. After the iron has reached the desired temperature, open and close the steam valve by pressing and releasing the valve. Hold the iron in a normal ironing position. Continue until all the water in the reservoir has been used up. Check for leaks during this procedure.

Does the iron still leak?

Yes—Proceed to **6210**.

No—Fault not verified. Iron has been used for too long as a dry iron.

6210

Steam chamber leaks

Step 1—The steam chamber is a hollow

space inside the sole plate. Water from the reservoir tank flows into this space when the steam button is operated and is quickly heated to steam. Refer to **5000** for disassembly of the iron and examine this area for leaks. If a leak is present, the iron is no longer useful as a steam iron, since the steam chamber is not a replaceable unit. The likelihood of this occurring is quite remote.

Does the steam chamber leak?

Yes—The iron is no longer serviceable as a steam iron, but it may be used as a dry iron.

No—Proceed to **6220**.

6220

Water release valve defective

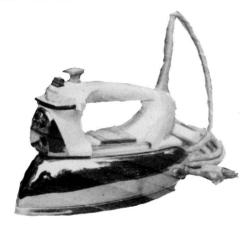

Fig. 19. Typical steam iron.

Step 1—Refer to **5000** and remove the handle to expose the water release valve. Make a simple sketch to help locate/arrange the parts for use in reassembly later. On most steam irons, as illustrated in Fig. 19, the handle is removed by prying up the nameplate with a screwdriver, etc. Usually two screws secure the handle to the iron. Remove these screws. Some irons have long screws which go through the upright portion of the handle. In still others the securing screws are reached through a removable part at the back of the handle. Proceed to Step 2.

Step 2—Examine the steam valve assembly to make sure the spring is under tension, is not broken, and that the needle is clean and not corroded. Also check the valve seat for roughness.

Do any of these conditions exist?

Yes—Obtain factory replacement parts. Take your damaged parts with you to the supplier to be sure you have an exact replacement. Proceed to Step 3.

No—Proceed to **6230**.

Step 3—Install the new valve assembly by following the removal steps in reverse order. Use the simple sketch previously made to help you remember the correct arrangement of parts. Test the iron after reassembly. Proceed to **6230** if the iron still leaks.

6230

Reservoir leaks

Step 1—When the handle is removed, access is easy to the screw that holds the top of the iron in place. Remove this screw and carefully lift the top off. It may be necessary to insert a sharp blade along the sole to pry the top loose. The water reservoir tank should drop out of the top of the iron. Proceed to Step 2.

Step 2—Examine the seams and the tank proper for discoloration.

This is usually an indication of leakage. Next, fill the tank with water and allow to stand. Check from time to time for leaks. Also check the gasket located between the sole plate and the tank for signs of leakage.

Are there any signs of leakage?

Yes—The tank and gasket must be replaced. Proceed to Step 3.

No—The cause of the leak has not been isolated. Carefully review the steps in **6200**.

Step 3—Obtain factory replacements for the necessary parts. Take the old parts with you to make certain the new parts are exact replacements. Proceed to Step 4.

Step 4—Reassemble the iron. Carefully position the tank over the sole plate. Make sure that the tank gasket is properly placed. Place the top of the iron over the tank and install the screw which holds it in place. Place the temperature actuating rod into the hole, making sure that the end engages the thermostat arm. Place a small amount of adhesive (obtainable from a parts distributor) around the neck of the filler assembly so that a seal is formed.

Step 5—Fill the iron with water and check for leaks and operation.

Does the iron operate normally; has the leak stopped?

Yes—The fault has been isolated and corrected.

No—You overlooked a step. Review **6200**.

IRON PRODUCES LITTLE OR NO STEAM

FAULT SYMPTOM 6300

Possible Causes:
- Steam ports on the sole are plugged _____ **See 6310**
- Valve stem on steam control inoperative _____ **See 6320**

6310

Steam ports on the sole are plugged

Step 1—Place a small piece of masking tape over each port on the sole of the iron when the iron is cold. Fill the iron with water. Now remove the tape from one port near the heel of the iron. Does water run out of the port? Replace the tape and expose a port at the tip or toe of the iron and then on each side.

Does water flow readily from the ports?

Yes—The steam ports are not plugged. Proceed to Step 2.

No—The steam ports are plugged. This part of the iron cannot be replaced. The iron is no longer serviceable as a steam iron. It may, of course, be used as a dry iron.

Step 2—Operate the iron dry at the highest temperature setting for 30 minutes, and then let it cool. Proceed to Step 3.

Step 3—Fill the iron with water and operate at the highest temperature setting while opening and closing the steam valve until the water is exhausted.

Does the iron generate steam in a satisfactory manner?

Yes—The fault has been isolated and corrected.

No—Proceed to **6320**.

6320

Valve stem on steam control inoperative

Step 1—Look into the filler hole while actuating the steam knob. If you can see the valve, is the valve stem rising and falling? If you cannot see the valve, proceed to Step 2.

Yes—Proceed to Step 3.

No—Proceed to Step 2.

Step 2—Remove the fastening screw

and remove the filler assembly. Remove the steam valve and examine the spring to see that it is not broken. Check the valve stem, and the tip especially, for evidence of damage (bent, broken, worn tip).

Did you observe any of these defects?

Yes—The fault may have been isolated. Proceed to Step 5.

No—Proceed to Step 3.

Step 3—Examine the valve seat in the tank to make sure the opening is not plugged or damaged.

Is the valve seat sealed or damaged?

Yes—Proceed to Step 4.

No—The fault has been isolated to a faulty valve stem. Proceed to Step 5.

Step 4—Attempt to clean out the port.

Were you able to accomplish this satisfactorily?

Yes—Proceed to Step 6.

No—The tank must be replaced. Proceed to Step 5.

Step 5—Obtain factory replacement parts. Take the old parts with you to be sure you get an exact replacement. Reassemble the valve and proceed to Step 6.

Step 6—Fill the iron with water and operate the steam control after allowing sufficient time for the iron to heat.

Did the iron generate a satisfactory amount of steam?

Yes—The fault has been isolated and repaired.

No—You have overlooked a step. Review the steps in **6300**.

NO SPRAY OR POOR SPRAY   FAULT SYMPTOM 6400

Possible Causes:

- Nozzle orifice plugged _____ **See 6410**
- Pump and nozzle assembly defective _____ **See 6420**

6410

Nozzle orifice plugged

Clean the nozzle assembly with a cleaning wire. A proper sized wire can be obtained from an authorized parts dealer. If you use a wire you have in your shop, be sure not to use one that is too large.

Does the spray operate satisfactorily?

Yes—The fault has been isolated and removed.

No—Proceed to **6420**.

6420

Pump and nozzle assembly defective

Step 1—Unplug and disassemble the iron and remove the pump. (Make a disassembly list.) Proceed to Step 2.

Step 2—Obtain a factory replacement pump and install the new pump. Follow your disassembly list in reverse order. Proceed to Step 3.

Step 3—Fill the iron with water and test the pump by operating it.

Does it spray satisfactorily?

Yes—Fault has been isolated and repaired.

No—Check over your installation; you overlooked something.

ELECTRIC OVEN/BROILER

OVEN WILL NOT HEAT

FAULT SYMPTOM 7000

Possible Causes:

- Defective cord set ⎯⎯⎯⎯⎯⎯⎯⎯⎯⎯⎯⎯⎯ **See 7010**
- Defective thermostat ⎯⎯⎯⎯⎯⎯⎯⎯⎯⎯⎯ **See 7020**
- Failed heating element ⎯⎯⎯⎯⎯⎯⎯⎯⎯⎯ **See 7030**

Initial Conditions Check List:

a. Plug a table lamp into the wall electric outlet to be sure you have a live circuit.
b. Plug the oven cord into the wall outlet and turn the oven control knob to the ON position.

Does the oven heat up?

Yes—Repeat a number of times. Allow the oven to cool between tests. You have not verified the fault. You must have overlooked an operating condition.

No—The fault is verified. Proceed to **7010**.

7010

Defective cord set

Step 1—Unplug the cord from the outlet. Examine the cord for breaks in the insulation, especially at the plug end.

Is the cord OK?

Yes—Proceed to Step 3.

No—The cord must be replaced. Proceed to Step 2.

CAUTION

DO NOT PROCEED BEFORE RE-MOVING THE CORD FROM THE WALL OUTLET.

CAUTION

Step 2—Turn the oven so that the side containing the temperature control is facing you. Note that while all ovens operate on the same principle, they do not all disassemble in the same manner. If the control knob has a set screw, loosen it and remove the knob. If there is no set screw, grasp the knob firmly and pull it off gently. Examine the plastic end piece for screws that hold it in place. They may be found around the edge, on the end outside the oven, or on the inside of the oven. Remove the screws and gently slide the plastic end off, taking care that the cord is not pulled excessively. Examine the cord connections.

Is the connection broken or insulation frayed?

Yes—Proceed to Step 4.

No—Proceed to Step 3.

Step 3—Turn the temperature control to OFF. Connect the alligator clamp of a test probe lamp to one prong of the cord plug (refer to Service Procedure **11000**) and touch the tip of the probe to the two connections inside the oven, one at a time. One of these should cause the lamp to glow. If neither one causes the test lamp to light, the cord is defective and must be replaced. If the lamp glows on one of these contacts, relocate the alligator clip to the other prong of the plug and repeat the test by touching the probe on the oven connection that did not previously cause the lamp to light.

Did the test lamp light in both cases?

NOTE:

Be sure the temperature control is in the OFF position.

Yes—The cord set is OK. Proceed to **7020**. Note that a cord that is burned or has badly frayed insulation inside the appliance should be replaced even if the tests with the test probe lamp were OK.

No—The cord is defective and must be replaced. Proceed to Step 4.

Step 4—Obtain a factory replacement cord set and install it. Reassemble the plastic end piece

and control knob. Reverse the procedure you followed in accomplishing Step 2. Proceed to Step 5.

Step 5—Plug the oven power cord into a live wall outlet and test the oven at various temperature settings.

Does the oven heat up?

Yes—The fault has been isolated and corrected.

No—Proceed to 7020.

7020

Defective thermostat

CAUTION

BE SURE THE PLUG IS REMOVED FROM THE WALL OUTLET.

CAUTION

Step 1—The temperature control knob is mounted on the shaft of the thermostat. Remove the temperature control knob and plastic end of the oven. See **7010** Step 2. Replace the knob on the shaft and rotate it counterclockwise until the unit clicks off. Connect the alligator clamp of a test light (Service Procedure **11000**) on one terminal at the base of the thermostat and touch the other terminal with the test probe. If the switch is in the OFF position the test lamp should not glow. Now turn the switch on. The test lamp should glow and as you rotate the knob to the highest temperature setting (clockwise) the test lamp should glow more brightly.

Does the test lamp remain off when the

switch is off and glow when the thermostat is turned ON?

Yes—The thermostat is OK. Proceed to **7030**.

No—The thermostat has failed and must be replaced. Proceed to Step 2.

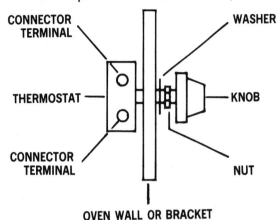

Fig. 20. Sketch of typical thermostat assembly.

Step 2—The thermostat is usually installed with a bracket and retained by a nut and washer that fits over the control shaft (see Fig. 20).

Use a soldering iron and heat the wires connected to the terminals. When the solder is fluid, pull the wire loose with a pair of pliers. If the wires are color coded, make a diagram of the connections for reference during reassembly. Now loosen the retaining nut with a pair of pliers or a wrench and remove the thermostat. Take this unit with you to be sure you obtain an exact replacement from your supplier.

Install the new thermostat in the exact reverse procedure you used in removing the defective one. Reassemble the plastic end piece, plug in the cord, and turn the switch on.

Does the oven heat up?

Yes—The fault has been isolated and corrected.

No—Check to be sure all connections are secure, the wall outlet is operative, and the switch on the oven is ON. If the oven still fails to operate, you have additional failed elements in the oven. Proceed to **7030**.

7030

Failed heating element

CAUTION

DO NOT PROCEED BEFORE REMOVING THE CORD FROM THE WALL OUTLET.

CAUTION

Heating elements come in two basic types. One is the nichrome wire wound to look like a coiled spring and mounted on standoff porcelain insulators. The other is the Calrod unit which looks like a tube approximately ¼ inch in diameter. Both types are installed beneath the top or above the bottom of the oven.

Step 1—Remove the control knob and plastic end piece (refer to **7010** Step 2). Carefully inspect the internal wiring that runs from the cord set to the thermostat, to the heating element, and back to the cord set. Look for broken or burned wires. If any are found they must be replaced. Before proceeding with that replacement, proceed to Step 2.

Step 2—Examine the heating element.

Is it the Nichrome Wire type?

Yes—Continue with Step 2.

No—Proceed to Step 5.

Step 2—(continued) Carefully inspect the wire elements. Use a good light. Look for missing pieces, breaks in the wire, or broken insulators. Remove the plastic end piece at the other end of the oven and inspect the wire connecting the two heating elements. If there are any breaks the heating element must be replaced. Never attempt a repair or to replace only one of the elements. The elements may be defective even though you have not observed obvious breaks. To locate these more subtle flaws attach the alligator clamp of a test lamp (Service Procedure **11000**) on one end of the heating element where it connects to the wiring at the thermostat. Touch the probe to the other end. If the lamp glows this portion of the heating element is OK. Now touch the test probe to the other connection of the element at the thermostat. If this section is OK the lamp will glow.

Does the lamp glow at both test points?

Yes—The heating element is OK. Proceed to Step 3.

No—The heating element is defective and must be replaced. Proceed to Step 4.

Step 3—If defective wires were found in Step 1 replace them with factory replacement parts. Reassemble and plug the oven cord set into an active outlet.

Does the oven operate?

Yes—The fault has been isolated and corrected.

No—Recheck your work looking especially for broken or insecure connections. The unit should work since all of the elements have been checked.

Step 4—Remove the heating element

and replace it with a factory replacement part. If any of the standoff insulators are broken or charred they should also be replaced. If the old heating element was connected to the oven by what appears to be a solder connection it is in fact a brazed joint. Extremely high temperature is needed to make such a connection. You can probably improvise a more conventional mechanical connection. In doing this BE SURE THE CONNECTION IS TIGHT AND DOES NOT CONTACT ANY PART OF THE OVEN. In no case use lead solder since it will melt and the connection will fail when the oven reaches operating temperatures. Reassemble and plug the oven cord set into an active outlet.

Does the oven operate satisfactorily?

Yes—The fault has been isolated and corrected.

No—Recheck your work looking especially for loose or poorly made connections. The unit should work since all of the units have been checked or replaced.

CAUTION

DO NOT PROCEED BEFORE REMOVING THE CORD FROM THE WALL OUTLET.

CAUTION

Step 5—Your oven is equipped with a calrod heating element. Examine it carefully in bright light for warping, cracks, and pitting. A crack is a definite indication of a failed element. Remove the plastic end piece at the other end of the oven and inspect the wire connecting the two heating elements. Faulty wiring on poor connections must be repaired. Before proceeding with this repair proceed to Step 6.

Step 6—Remove the plastic support at the end opposite from that containing the thermostat. Examine the wire that connects the two calrod units for breaks. A broken wire may be replaced. Attach the alligator clamp of a test light (Service Procedure **11000**) on the calrod terminal where it connects with the thermostat. Touch the probe to the other end of the calrod. Now place the probe on the end of the second element. In both tests the lamp will glow if the calrods are OK.

Does the lamp light on both tests?

Yes—The calrod elements are OK. Proceed to Step 7.

No—The calrod is defective and must be replaced. Proceed to Step 8.

Step 7—If defective wires or connections were found in Step 5, replace them with factory equivalent parts. Reassemble and plug the oven into an active outlet.

Does the oven operate?

Yes—The fault has been isolated and corrected.

No—Recheck your work looking especially for broken or insecure connections. The unit should work since all of the elements have been checked.

Step 8—Remove and replace the calrod units with factory replacement parts. Always replace both units.

NOTE:

If the old element was connected to the oven by what appears to be a solder connection it is in fact a brazed joint. Extremely high temperature is needed to make such a connection. You can probably improvise a more conventional mechanical connection. In doing this BE SURE THE CONNECTION IS TIGHT AND DOES NOT CONTACT ANY PART OF THE OVEN. In no case use lead solder since it will melt and the connection will fail when the oven reaches operating temperatures. Reassemble and plug the oven cord set into an active outlet.

Does the oven operate satisfactorily?

Yes—The fault has been isolated and corrected.

No—Recheck your work looking especially for loose or poorly made connections. The oven should work since all of the units have been checked or replaced.

OVEN DOES NOT REACH MAXIMUM TEMPERATURE WITH CONTROL AT HIGH SETTING FAULT SYMPTOM 7100

Possible Causes:

- Tired heating element _____ **See 7110**
- Defective control unit _____ **See 7120**

7110

Tired heating element

CAUTION

THIS NEXT STEP INVOLVES A TEST THAT REQUIRES THE OVEN TO BE PLUGGED INTO THE HOUSE'S ELECTRIC POWER SUPPLY. EXERCISE GREAT CAUTION. FOR SAFETY, PLACE ALL TOOLS OUT OF REACH. DO NOT PUT YOUR HANDS INSIDE THE OVEN. DO NOT TOUCH THE HEATING ELEMENTS. DO NOT CONDUCT THE TEST NEAR WATER OR A SINK.

CAUTION

Step 1—Place the oven on its back or in any position that will allow a clear view of the heating element. Insert the oven power cord into a live wall outlet. Set the oven control at the highest setting and wait for the unit to come to its maximum temperature. In an oven that is operating normally the heating elements will have an even cherry-red glow. There should be no dark areas.

Does the element have a uniform cherry-red glow?

Yes—The fault is not related to a deficiency in the element. Proceed to Fault Symptom **7120**.

No—The heating element is defective. Unplug the oven and allow it to cool. Remove and replace the defective heating element as described in **7030** Step 4 or 8 depending on the type of element.

NOTE:

If the heating elements do not get red at all, the problem may be in the thermostat. Proceed to Fault Symptom **7120**.

7120

Defective control unit

CAUTION

REMOVE THE PLUG FROM THE WALL OUTLET. BEFORE PROCEEDING, ALLOW THE OVEN TO COOL.

CAUTION

Step 1—Disassemble and check the thermostat as described in **7020** Step 1. The critical test is the one in which you turn on the control switch and rotate it through its full range. The test lamp should glow and increase in brightness as the control is moved to higher temperature settings if it is operating as it should.

Does the test light increase in brightness as the control is moved to higher temperature settings?

Yes—The fault has not been verified. Repeat the test a number of times. If the tests give the same result and the elements are cherry-red your oven is operating as designed.

No—The thermostat must be replaced. Refer to **7020** Step 2 for replacement procedures.

BROILER/ROTISSERIE

UNIT WILL NOT HEAT

FAULT SYMPTOM 8000

Possible Causes:

- Defective cord set _____ **See 8010**
- Defective heating element _____ **See 8020**

Initial Conditions Check List:

a. Plug a table lamp into the wall electric outlet to be sure you have a live circuit.
b. Plug the broiler into the live wall outlet.

Does the broiler heat?

Yes—If the broiler heats up satisfactorily after a number of trials in which the unit was allowed to cool between trials the fault has not been verified.

No—Proceed to **8010**.

8010

Defective cord set

Step 1—Unplug the cord set from the wall outlet and then from the broiler. Examine the cord for breaks in the insulation especially at the terminal ends. Inspect the plug end that is inserted into the appliance for pitting and deep blue/black burn marks.

Is the cord set in apparently good condition?

Yes—The fault has not yet been isolated. Proceed to Step 2.

No—Replace the cord set and proceed to Step 3.

Step 2—Check the cord set with a test light to determine if there are breaks in the line that are invisible. Refer to Service Procedure **11000**-2(b) for this test.

Is the test cord OK?

Yes—The fault is not with the cord set. Proceed to **8020**.

No—The cord set must be replaced. Be sure to obtain an identical factory replacement. Proceed to Step 3.

Step 3—Connect the cord set to the broiler and then insert the plug in a live wall outlet.

Does the broiler function normally?

Yes—The fault has been found and repaired.

No—There are additional problems with your broiler. Proceed to **8020.**

8020

Defective heating element

CAUTION

DO NOT PROCEED BEFORE REMOVING THE CORD SET FROM THE WALL OUTLET.

CAUTION

Unless you have a very old unit your broiler/rotisserie will have a calrod heating element. Proceed to Step 1.

Step 1—Examine the element carefully in bright light for warping, cracks, and pitting. A crack is a definite indication of a failed element. Attach the alligator clamp of a test light (Service Procedure **11000**) to one of the calrod terminals. Touch the tip of the probe to the other end. The test light should glow.

Does the test light glow?

Yes—The calrod is OK. Recheck the connecting plug at the end of the cord set. The fault is probably at that end.

No—The calrod is defective and needs to be replaced. Obtain a factory repair part and install. Your broiler should be OK.

BROILER/ROTISSERIE DOES NOT REACH MAXIMUM TEMPERATURE FAULT SYMPTOM 8100

Possible Cause:

- Tired heating element _____ **See 8110**

8110

Tired heating element

CAUTION

THIS TEST REQUIRES THE UNIT TO BE PLUGGED INTO THE HOUSE'S ELECTRIC POWER SUPPLY. EXERCISE GREAT CARE. DO NOT TOUCH THE ELEMENT. DO NOT CONDUCT TEST NEAR WATER OR ON A COUNTER TOP NEAR A SINK.

CAUTION

Step 1—Place the oven so that you have a clear view of the heating element. Insert the power cord into a live wall outlet and wait for the unit to develop its maximum temperature. It should be cherry-red in about two minutes. There should be no dark spots or areas.

Does the element have a uniform cherry-red glow?

Yes—The fault has not been verified.

No—The heating element is defective. Unplug power cord. Remove the heating element and replace it with a factory replacement part. The broiler will operate like new.

UNIT HEATS BUT ROTISSERIE MOTOR DOES NOT OPERATE
FAULT SYMPTOM 8200

Possible Causes:
- Defective cord set _____ **See 8210**
- Switch inoperative _____ **See 8220**
- Motor has failed _____ **See 8230**

Initial Conditions Check List:

a. Plug a table lamp into the wall electric outlet to be sure you have a live circuit.
b. Examine the square opening on the motor shaft into which the rotisserie spear is inserted. If there is an accumulation of dried and hardened fat, scrape this away and clean the surface with an ammonia solution. Be sure the shaft can be rotated; turn it with your fingers. Sparingly apply a very light machine oil to the shaft.
c. Plug the unit into the live wall outlet and turn on the motor switch.

Does the motor operate?

Yes—The fault is not verified. You overlooked an initial condition.

No—Proceed to **8210**.

8210

Defective cord set

Step 1—Inspect the cord set for frayed or defective insulation. Check the prongs for looseness.

Is the cord set OK?

Yes—Proceed to Step 4. The fault has not yet been found.

No—The cord set must be replaced. Proceed to Step 2.

CAUTION

BEFORE PROCEEDING, BE SURE THE POWER CORD HAS BEEN REMOVED FROM THE WALL OUTLET.

CAUTION

Step 2—Withdraw the retaining screws on the front or rear of the motor assembly to expose the leads from the power cord. One lead goes to the motor and the other to the switch. Remove the connector to the motor and the one to the switch. Install a factory replacement power cord. Be sure to make the connections secure. Proceed to Step 3.

Step 3—Reassemble the motor unit and plug the unit into a live wall outlet. Turn on the switch.

Does the motor operate?

Yes—The fault has been isolated and repaired.

No—Proceed to **8220**.

Step 4—Expose the attachments of the cord set as described in Step 2. With the cord set detached and unplugged from the wall, test the cord with a test light. (See Service Procedure **11000**.) Attach the alligator clip to one of the terminal leads and touch the probe to one of the prongs of the cord set plug. Does the light glow? Now touch the other prong. Does the light glow? The light should glow only at one of the prongs. Now move the alligator clip to the other terminal. The prong that did not produce a light before should do so now.

Did the test perform as described?

Yes—The cord is OK. Proceed to **8220**.

No—The power cord must be replaced. Refer to Step 2.

8220

Switch inoperative

CAUTION

BE SURE TO UNPLUG THE POWER CORD.

CAUTION

Step 1—Withdraw the retaining screws on the front or rear of the motor assembly to expose the leads and switch. Remove the solderless connector lead between the switch and the motor. Using a test light attach the alligator clamp on one wire of the switch and the probe on the other. Turn the switch ON and OFF.

Does the test light go on and off?

Yes—The switch is OK. If you have done the previous tests correctly and eliminated them as causes of failure there is only one possible cause left—the motor has failed. Proceed to **8230**.

No—Replace the switch with a factory replacement part and reassemble. Proceed to Step 2.

Step 2—Plug the motor into a live outlet and turn the switch ON.

Does the motor run?

Yes—Fault has been isolated and repaired.

No—In addition to a faulty switch you appear to have a failed motor. Proceed to **8230**.

8230

Motor has failed

There is no simple test you can perform to check out the motor. Take it to an appliance repair shop for inspection. A repair job or a factory replacement motor will be expensive. Only you can judge based on the value of the unit, whether such an investment is justified.

Step 1—If a motor replacement is decided on, install and reassemble. Be sure all connections are secure. Proceed to Step 2.

Step 2—Plug the unit into a live wall outlet and turn on the switch.

Does the motor operate?

Yes—The fault has been isolated and repaired.

No—Recheck your previous work. There must be a loose connection or faulty power cord.

SPACE HEATER

UNIT WILL NOT HEAT

FAULT SYMPTOM 9000

Possible Causes:

- Defective power cord ————————————— **See 9010**
- Internal wire assembly defective ——————— **See 9020**
- Defective thermostat ——————————————— **See 9030**
- Defective heating element ————————————— **See 9040**

Initial Conditions Check List:

a. Plug a table lamp into the wall outlet to be sure you have a live circuit.
b. Plug the Space Heater cord set into the wall outlet and turn the switch first to LOW, later to MEDIUM and still later to HIGH. Does the heater come on and become increasingly hot? Repeat this a number of times.

Yes—The fault is not verified. One of the initial conditions must have been overlooked.

No—Proceed to **9010**.

9010

Defective power cord

CAUTION

UNPLUG THE POWER CORD FROM THE WALL OUTLET.

CAUTION

Step 1—Examine the cord set for fraying and broken insulation. Inspect the plug to make certain the connection to the prongs is sound and that the prongs are not loose.

Does the cord set appear to be in satisfactory condition?

Yes—Proceed to Step 2.

No—The cord must be replaced. Proceed to Step 3.

Step 2—Turn the heater so that the side containing the temperature control and switch faces you. While all space heaters operate on the same principle they are of differing shapes and sizes and are assembled in different ways. Inspect your heater carefully before you start taking it apart. Begin by removing the control knob. If the control knob has a set screw, loosen it and remove the knob. If there is no set screw, grasp the knob firmly and pull it gently until it comes off. Now examine the heater along the bottom and sides for small screws that secure the front and/or back panels of the heater case. Remove these screws and remove the panel(s). Carefully examine the connections where the cord set attaches to the internal wire assembly for broken or burned wires. Check the cord set with a test light. Turn the temperature control to the OFF position. Connect the alligator clamp of the test probe lamp to one prong of the cord plug. Refer to Service Procedure **11000** and touch the tip of the probe to the two connections inside the heater, one at a time. One of these should cause the lamp to glow. If neither one glows the cord is defective and must be replaced. If the lamp glowed on one of these contacts relocate the alligator clip to the other prong of the power cord and repeat the test by touching the probe to the heater connection that did not previously cause the test lamp to glow.

Did the test lamp glow in both tests?

Yes—The cord set is OK. Proceed to **9020**. A cord that is burned or badly frayed inside the appliance should be replaced even though the tests with the test light were OK. If this is the case proceed to Step 3.

No—The cord is defective and must be replaced. Proceed to Step 3.

Step 3—Obtain a factory replacement cord set and install it. Reassemble the heater by performing the operations in reverse

order that were necessary for disassembly. Plug the heater power cord into a live wall outlet, turn on the switch, and test the heater at various temperature settings.

Does the heater operate normally?

Yes—The fault has been isolated and corrected.

No—Proceed to **9020**.

9020

Internal wire assembly defective

CAUTION

REMOVE THE POWER CORD FROM THE WALL OUTLET

CAUTION

NOTE:
Space heaters with forced air blowers come in two types.
a. One type has a variable resistor used to adjust the heat level and a 3-speed switch to regulate the speed of the motor.
b. Another type is found in less expensive models which provide only one heat level and a 2- or 3-speed switch to regulate the blower output. To isolate the fault symptoms for Type b follow the procedures for Type a but disregard the steps for testing the variable resistor.

Step 1—Remove the back or front of the case as described in **9010** Step 2. Examine the wire assembly inside the frame. Look for frayed or burned insulation. Gently move each wire to test the security of each connection. Test each wire from connection to connection with a test lamp to be sure there are no hidden breaks. Refer to Service Procedure **11000**.

Are any of the wires loose or broken? Is the insulation frayed or burned?

Yes—Resolder or replace wires as required. Proceed to Step 2.

NOTE:
Always replace a wire lead with a new wire that has the same resistance value and insulation type. Never use ordinary rubber insulated wire.

No—The fault has not been isolated. Proceed to **9030**.

Step 2—Reassemble the heater and plug the cord into a live wall outlet. Turn on the switch and test the heater at various settings.

Does the heater function normally?

Yes—The fault has been isolated and repaired.

No—Proceed to **9030**.

9030

Defective thermostat

CAUTION

REMOVE THE HEATER POWER CORD FROM THE WALL OUTLET.

CAUTION

Step 1—Remove the front or rear panel of the heater as described in **9010** Step 2. Adjust the control knob to the highest temperature setting. Attach the alligator clamp of a test light to one of

the thermostat terminal leads; touch the tip of the probe to the other lead. If the probe light glows, the thermostat is OK. As the control is turned to lower settings the brightness of the light should decrease and at the lowest level it might go out.

Does the thermostat operate normally?

Yes—The fault has not been isolated. Proceed to **9040**.

No—The thermostat is defective and must be replaced. Proceed to Step 2.

Step 2—Disconnect the leads from the thermostat. Remove the control knob on the front panel. You will either loosen a set screw in the knob or gently pull it off depending on the type on your heater. Remove the hex nut and escutcheon. This releases the thermostat. Install a factory replacement part. Take the faulty thermostat with you when you make the purchase. Reconnect the wires you removed earlier and reassemble the heater. Proceed to Step 3.

Step 3—Plug the heater power cord into a live wall outlet and turn on the heater; rotate the switch through the range—LOW, MEDIUM, and HIGH.

Does the heater come on and operate over the full range?

Yes—The fault has been isolated and repaired.

No—Proceed to **9040**.

9040

Defective heating element

Heating elements come in two basic types.

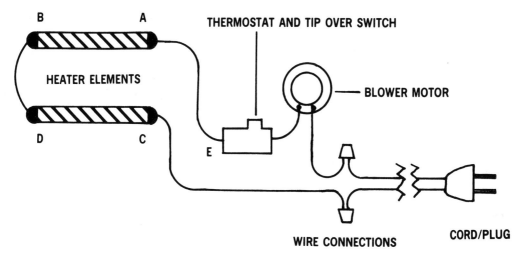

Fig. 21. Circuit schematic.

a. Nichrome wire is wound like a coiled spring and mounted around or on standoff porcelain insulators.

b. Calrod units which look like tubes are approximately ¼ inch in diameter and can be shaped to any configuration.

CAUTION

REMOVE THE POWER CORD FROM THE WALL OUTLET.

CAUTION

Step 1—Remove the front or rear panel of the heater as described in **9010** Step 2. Inspect the heating element in bright light. Look for breaks in the wire or cracks in the rod. Move the element gently during your test.

Did you find any breaks or cracks?

Yes—The heating element is defective and must be replaced. Proceed to Step 2.

No—You have not yet established the condition of the heating element.

Proceed to Step 3.

Step 2—Obtain a factory replacement part. Remove the old element(s) and install the new one following the reverse procedure. You will find it helpful to make a diagram and sequence of operations in accomplishing this task. Be sure that all connections are secure and that the insulators are properly installed. Check your work carefully. Reassemble the entire unit and plug the power cord into a live wall outlet. Turn on the control.

Does the heat come on?

Yes—The fault has been isolated and repaired.

No—Recheck your work. Look especially for loose or poorly made connections. The heater should work since all of the units have been checked or repaired.

Step 3—Use a test light to check out the condition of the heating element. Place the alligator clamp on one terminal of the element (at Point A, Fig. 21) and the probe on the other (Point B). Test each element individually (A to B, then C to D). Now test the total system by placing the alligator clamp on the connection from the temperature control, E, and the probe on the last element in the circuit, C.

Does the lamp glow on all tests?

Yes—While this test indicates the elements are functional it is not a perfect test of the condition of the element. Small cracks or breaks in the element may not show up until the element starts to heat up and then fails. If this is the case you should get intermittent operation. The unit should start to get warm and then quit.

No—If none of the above works recheck your earlier work. You must have missed a failure in another part. If all steps were covered proceed to **9100**.

UNIT DOES NOT REACH MAXIMUM TEMPERATURE

FAULT SYMPTOM 9100

Possible Causes:

- Defective heating element _____ **See 9110**
- Defective thermostat _____ **See 9120**

CAUTION

THIS TEST MUST BE PERFORMED WITH THE HOUSE 110-VOLT POWER ON. DO NOT TOUCH THE HEATER DURING THIS TEST, NOR CONDUCT IT NEAR A SINK.

CAUTION

9110

Defective heating element

Step 1—Place the heater in a position where the heating elements may be observed without getting your face too close. Plug the heater cord into a live wall outlet and turn it to its highest setting. Allow the heater to reach its highest temperature. When this has occurred, visually examine the heating elements. They should all be bright cherry-red with no dark spots.

Does the heating element have a uniform cherry-red glow?

Yes—The fault is not related to a deficiency in the element(s). You may be expecting more than the heater is capable of. If you can, compare your heater with a new one of the same type. Proceed to **9120** to check the control unit (thermostat).

No—The heating element(s) are defective and need to be replaced. Refer to **9040** to accomplish this repair. If the elements do not get red at all, proceed to **9120**.

9120

Defective thermostat

CAUTION

REMOVE THE HEATER POWER CORD FROM THE WALL OUTLET.

CAUTION

Step 1—Remove the heater case as described in **9010** Step 2 and perform the tests with the test light as indicated.

Does the thermostat check out OK?

Yes—The fault has not been isolated.

The most likely cause is a deficient heating element. Recheck **9110**.

No—The fault is isolated to the thermostat. Remove and replace the thermostat as described in **9030.**

HEATER WORKS—BLOWER DOES NOT

FAULT SYMPTOM 9200

Possible Causes:

- Fan blade is loose _____ **See 9210**
- Internal wire is broken _____ **See 9220**
- Switch has failed _____ **See 9230**
- Motor has failed _____ **See 9240**

CAUTION

UNPLUG THE HEATER FROM THE WALL OUTLET.

CAUTION

9210

Fan blade is loose

Step 1—Remove the case of the heater as described in **9010** Step 2. Examine the blade on the motor shaft to determine if it is securely fastened to the shaft.

Is the fan blade secure?

Yes—The fault has not been isolated. Proceed to **9220**.

No—Secure the blade firmly to the shaft. Locate it so that it will not shake any fixed parts of the heater. Proceed to Step 2.

Step 2—Reassemble the unit and plug the heater power cord into the wall outlet. Turn on the switch.

Does the fan operate?

Yes—The fault has been isolated and corrected.

No—The fault has not been found. Proceed to **9220**.

9220

Internal wire is broken

CAUTION

REMOVE THE POWER CORD FROM THE WALL OUTLET.

CAUTION

Step 1—Remove the case of the heater as described in **9010** Step 2. Check the wires to the switch and from the switch to the motor. Look for frayed or broken wires. Gently move each wire to test the security of the connections. Test each wire from connection to connection with a test lamp to be sure there are no hidden breaks. Refer to Service Procedure **11000.**

Are any of the wires loose or broken? Is the insulation frayed or burned?

Yes—Repair the broken wires or replace as needed. Proceed to Step 2.

No—The fault has not been isolated. Proceed to **9230.**

Step 2—Reassemble the heater and plug the unit into a live wall outlet.

Does the fan operate?

Yes—The fault has been isolated and corrected.

No—Proceed to **9230.**

9230

Switch has failed

CAUTION

REMOVE THE POWER CORD FROM THE WALL OUTLET.

CAUTION

Step 1—Remove the case of the heater as described in **9010** Step 2. Use a probe light tester to check the switch. Connect the alligator clamp of the test light to one of the terminals on the switch and touch the other terminal with the test probe. When the switch is in the OFF position your test light should not glow. Now turn the switch ON. The test lamp should glow and

as you rotate the control to the highest speed the test lamp should glow more brightly.

Does the test lamp remain OFF and glow more brightly as the control is advanced?

Yes—The fault is not isolated. Proceed to **9240.**

No—The fault is with the switch which must be replaced. Proceed to Step 2.

Step 2—Remove the switch and install a factory replacement part. Proceed to Step 3.

Step 3—Reassemble the heater. Be sure to check that all connections are secure and in accordance with the original hookup. Plug the appliance into a live outlet.

Does the fan operate?

Yes—The fault has been isolated and repaired.

No—Proceed to **9240.**

9240

Motor has failed

CAUTION

UNPLUG THE UNIT FROM THE WALL OUTLET.

CAUTION

Step 1—Try to rotate the fan blade with your finger.

Does it move freely?

Yes—Fault has not been found. Proceed to Step 2.

No—Fault may be isolated. Proceed to Step 3.

Step 2—Examine the fan and motor shaft for metal dust or particles.

Did you find dust or particles?

Yes—The bearing has probably failed. This is not a definitive test, however. You could remove the motor and have it checked at an electrical repair shop. The cost of repair or replacement, if it has failed and this is most likely, approximates the cost of a new unit. You will have to decide based on the age, appearance, etc., of your heater if the investment is worth it.

No—You will be unable to check the motor further in your home shop. Remove it and take it to an electric repair shop. Keep in mind that a repair or new motor will cost almost as much as a new heater.

Step 3—Look for an oil port at each end of the fan motor. If you find them, lubricate sparingly (a drop or two of very light oil). Rotate the fan a number of times.

Does it run more freely?

Yes—Proceed to Step 4.

No—The motor has probably failed. See comments in Step 2.

Step 4—Assemble the unit and plug the power cord into an active outlet. Turn on the unit.

Does the motor operate?

Yes—Fault is isolated and corrected. Remember to oil the motor occasionally.

No—Motor has undoubtedly failed. See comments in Step 2.

HAIR DRYER

DRYER WILL NOT HEAT AND MOTOR IS INOPERATIVE
FAULT SYMPTOM 10000

Possible Causes:

- Defective cord set ————————————— **See 10010**
- Internal wiring loose or broken ——————— **See 10010**
- Defective switch ———————————————— **See 10020**
- Motor and heater are both defective ————— **See 10030**

Initial Conditions Check List:

a. Plug a table lamp into the wall power outlet to be sure it is alive.

b. Plug the dryer into the wall outlet and turn on the switch; activate it through HIGH and LOW.

Does the motor run and the dryer heat?

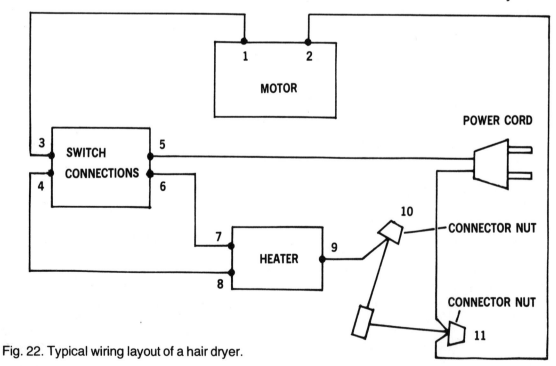

Fig. 22. Typical wiring layout of a hair dryer.

Yes—The fault was not verified. You must have plugged it into a dead outlet or neglected to turn on the switch.

No—The fault is verified. Unplug the dryer and proceed to **10010**.

10010

Defective cord set

Step 1—Examine the cord set for wear such as broken or cracked insulation where wire enters the plug and the dryer.

Are the prongs securely bonded into the plug? Is the cord in acceptable condition?

Yes—Proceed to Step 2.

No—The power cord must be replaced. Proceed to Step 4.

CAUTION

REMOVE POWER CORD FROM OUTLET.

CAUTION

Step 2—Remove the control knob. The knob is retained either by a set screw or by a force fit. In the latter case simply grasp the knob and pull it off gently.
Withdraw the latch screw if the unit has a hard plastic hood. Disregard if the hood is a soft bonnet. Now withdraw the base screws (there are usually four of these) and lift the case deck assembly from the case bottom. If the switch is attached to the case deck, remove the retaining screws (there are usually two) to release the switch.

Examine the internal wires of the power cord which connect to the heater, the motor, and the switch.

Are any of these wires loose or broken?

Yes—Repair the broken or loose connections. Proceed to Step 3 and check the power cord.

No—Proceed to Step 3.

Step 3—Remove one of the plastic electric nuts and using a test light probe check the continuity between this connection and one of the prongs of the power cord. Using a test light which has one leg with an alligator clip, fasten the clip to the exposed connection and touch the other test probe to one of the flat prongs of the power cord and then to the other prong.

NOTE:

The power cord plug usually has three prongs. The center one is usually round and is the safety-case ground plug. Do not use this prong in this test. One of these actions should cause the test light to glow. As a final check attach the alligator clip to the prong which did not cause the light to glow. Now touch the probe to the power line cord at the point where the cord connects to the opposite side of the switch.

Did the test light glow for both of these tests?

Yes—The cord set and its internal connections are OK. Proceed to Fault Symptom **10020**.

No—The cord set is defective and should be replaced with one of equivalent specifications. Proceed to Step 4.

Step 4—Carefully disconnect the power cord from the unit noting carefully where each wire is attached. (Making a diagram of the attachment points is a helpful aid.) Install the new wire. Before assembling and testing proceed to Step 5.

Step 5—Using a test light check the continuity of the wire going between the switch and the motor, the switch and the heating element, the motor and the ground return, and the heater and the ground return.

Does the lamp glow on each of these wire continuity tests?

Yes—All the internal wires and connections are OK. Proceed to Step 6.

No—Remove and replace the defective wire with exactly the same type and specification wire. Your appliance dealer can sell you this wire. Proceed to Step 6.

Step 6—Reassemble the unit and plug the dryer into an active wall outlet. Turn on the heater switch and rotate it from HIGH to LOW.

Does the dryer operate normally?

Yes—The fault has been isolated and repaired.

No—The fault is elsewhere in the dryer. Proceed to **10020**.

10020

Defective switch

CAUTION

REMOVE THE PLUG FROM THE WALL OUTLET BEFORE PROCEEDING.

CAUTION

Step 1—Open up the dryer case to gain access to the interior of the dryer. Refer to **10010** Step 2. Using a test light attach the alligator clip to the power input side of the switch. Touch the probe on the lead to the motor contact, the low temperature heat lead, and the high temperature heat lead in sequence. Operate the switch from OFF to ON as you perform each test.

Does the test light glow in all control positions?

Yes—You may have overlooked something in the previous tests. Check your work. If you still get an OK the fault is with the motor, the heater, or both. Proceed to Fault Symptom **10030**.

No—The switch is defective. Proceed to Step 2.

Step 2—Replace the switch with a factory replacement part. Be sure that all connections are correctly made and are secure. It's a good idea to make a wiring diagram before you remove the leads to the old switch. Assemble the dryer and plug it into a live wall outlet. Turn the dryer on and move the switch through the full range.

Does the dryer operate normally?

Yes—The fault has been isolated and corrected.

No—Check your work to be sure the connections are properly made and secure. If the dryer still fails to operate you probably have a failed motor and a heating element. See Fault Symptom **10030**.

10030

Motor and heater are both defective

Since you have checked the continuity of power flow from the power cord through the switch to the motor, and through the motor return to the ground (Fault Symptom **10010** Steps 2 through 6), the probability of motor and heater failure is extremely high since all the other possible causes have been eliminated. Before you make this decision, check your work again to be sure you did not overlook something.

Step 1—Investigate the cost of a replacement motor and heating element. You may find the repair is not justified based on the age and condition of your dryer as compared to the cost of a new one. If you decide to replace them proceed to Fault Symptom **10130** Step 2 and Fault Symptom **10230**.

HEATER ELEMENT WORKS BUT MOTOR DOES NOT RUN
FAULT SYMPTOM 10100

Possible Causes:

- Impeller is jammed _____ **See 10110**
- Wiring loose or broken _____ **See 10120**
- Motor has failed _____ **See 10130**

10110

Impeller is jammed

Step 1—Disassemble the dryer as described in **10010** Step 2. Remove the inner deck assembly by removing the retaining screws and lifting it from the lower portion of the case. Try to rotate the impeller.

Does it move freely?

Yes— Proceed to Fault Symptom **10120**.

No—Clear the well of any foreign material. Straighten any bent or warped edges of the impeller. Proceed to Step 2.

Step 2—Reassemble the dryer and plug it into a live wall plug. Turn on the dryer.
Does the motor operate?

Yes—The fault has been isolated and repaired.

No—Proceed to Fault Symptom **10120**.

10120

Wiring loose or broken

Step 1—Disassemble the dryer as described in **10010** Step 2. Check the internal wiring from the switch to the motor for loose or broken connections and with the test light as described in Fault Symptom **10010** Step 3. Tighten loose wires and install new ones as necessary. Reassemble, plug into an active outlet, and turn the dryer on.

Does the motor run?

Yes—The fault has been isolated and corrected.

No—Proceed to Fault Symptom **10130**.

10130

Motor has failed

Since you have checked the continuity of

power flow from the power cord through the switch to the motor and through the motor return to ground (Fault Symptom **10010** Steps 2 through 6), the probability of a motor failure is extremely high since you have eliminated all other possible faults.

Step 1—Investigate what it will cost to repair or replace the motor. You may find the cost is not justified based on the age and condition of your dryer as compared with the cost of a new dryer. If you decide to replace the motor proceed to Step 2.

CAUTION

REMOVE THE POWER CORD FROM THE WALL OUTLET BEFORE PROCEEDING.

CAUTION

Step 2—Withdraw the screws that hold the inner case deck assembly and separate it from the case bottom. Remove the wire leads that connect the switch to the motor and the motor ground. Proceed to Step 3.

Step 3—Remove the impeller from the motor. The impeller may be held fast by a spring retaining ring or clip, or it may just be a press fit. If it is a press fit, warm the impeller with a soldering iron. Hold the iron on or near the shaft until the plastic becomes pliable and then slip it off the shaft. NOTE: If you had to heat the impeller to remove it you will need a replacement when you reassemble the dryer. Proceed to Step 4.

Step 4—Remove the motor from the base plate by removing the retaining screws. Take the base plate and the old motor to the local appliance center and purchase a factory replacement part or equivalent. If you need a new impeller, have the service center press fit the new impeller to the motor shaft. If you have any doubts about the condition of the motor the service center has the capability of checking it out. Proceed to Step 5.

Step 5—Install the motor and reassemble the unit in the reverse order of disassembly. Check all the connections to be sure they are correct and secure. Proceed to Step 6.

Step 6—Plug the dryer into an active wall outlet and turn on the dryer.

Does it operate normally?

Yes—The fault has been isolated and corrected.

No—Recheck your assembly diagram. You made an incorrect or poor connection.

MOTOR RUNS BUT DRYER DOES NOT HEAT

FAULT SYMPTOM 10200

Possible Causes:

- Internal wiring loose or broken _____ **See 10210**
- Switch has failed _____ **See 10220**
- Heating element has failed _____ **See 10230**

10210

Internal wiring loose or broken

CAUTION

REMOVE THE POWER CORD FROM THE WALL OUTLET.

CAUTION

Step 1—Disassemble the unit as described in Fault Symptom **10010** Step 2 and check the internal wiring from the switch to the heater to determine if there are any loose or broken wires.

Did you find such problems?

Yes—The fault may have been isolated. Proceed to Step 2.

No—Proceed to Step 3.

Step 2—Fasten or replace the wires as needed, reassemble, and plug into an active outlet. Turn on the dryer.

Does it heat up?

Yes—Fault is isolated and repaired.

No—Proceed to Step 3.

CAUTION

REMOVE POWER CORD.

CAUTION

Step 3—Use a test light to check the leads from the switch to the heater element. Follow service procedure **11000**.

Does the test light glow?

Yes—You have not found the fault yet. Proceed to Fault Symptom **10220**.

No—The fault may have been found. Remove and replace the broken lead. Proceed to Step 4.

Step 4—Plug the dryer into an active wall outlet and turn it on.

Does it heat up?

Yes—The fault has been found and fixed.

No—Proceed to **10220**.

10220

Switch has failed

CAUTION

UNPLUG THE DRYER FROM THE WALL OUTLET.

CAUTION

Step 1—Disassemble the dryer as indicated in Fault Symptom **10010** Step 2. Use a test light and check the switch by attaching the alligator clip to the power input side of the switch. Touch the probe on the lead to the motor contact, the low temperature heat lead, and the high temperature heat lead in sequence. Operate the switch from OFF to ON as you perform each test.

Does the test light glow in all control positions?

Yes—The switch is OK. You have not found the fault yet. Proceed to Fault Symptom **10230**.

No—The switch is defective. Proceed to Step 2.

Step 2—Replace the switch with a fac-

tory replacement part. Be sure all connections are correctly made and secure. It is a good idea to make a wiring diagram before you remove the old switch. Assemble the dryer and plug it into an active wall plug. Turn the dryer ON and rotate the switch through the full range.

Does the dryer operate normally?

Yes—The fault has been isolated and corrected.

No—Proceed to Fault Symptom **10230**.

10230

Heating element has failed

NOTE:

If you have completely and carefully checked the continuity of the wires as described in **10210** and **10220** and found everything in order it is very likely that the heating element has failed.

CAUTION

REMOVE THE POWER CORD FROM THE WALL OUTLET.

CAUTION

Step 1—Disassemble the dryer as described in Fault Symptom **10010** Step 2 and check the nichrome wires (coiled wires in the heater) for breaks or badly eroded or pitted areas. Even if the element looks OK check it out with your test light. Attach the alligator clip to one end of the coil and touch the probe to the other end. If the wire is defective or the test light fails to glow, the element is defective.

Is the coil OK?

Yes—The unit should heat. You must have missed a step in the previous test. Recheck your work.

No—Disconnect the heating element and replace it with a replacement part. Proceed to Step 2.

Step 2—Reassemble the dryer and plug it into an active wall outlet. Rotate the control through the full range.

Does the dryer operate normally?

Yes—The fault has been found and corrected.

No—You overlooked a step along the way. Recheck your work.

MOTOR AND HEATER WORK BUT WARM AIR DOES NOT ENTER THE HOOD   FAULT SYMPTOM 10300

Possible Causes:

- Filter is fouled _____ **See 10310**
- Heat duct or hose is plugged _____ **See 10320**
- Impeller loose _____ **See 10330**

10310

Filter is fouled

Step 1—Gently pry off the air inlet screen usually located on top of the case assembly. The filter is directly beneath the screen. Remove the filter and wash it in a mild detergent. Replace the filter when it has dried. Reassemble and plug into the house wall outlet. Turn on the dryer and operate the control through the full range.

Is the air flow restored?

Yes—The fault has been found and fixed.

No—Proceed to **10320**.

10320

Heat duct or hose is plugged

Step 1—Remove the hood ring assembly. Remove the deck assembly as described in **10010** Step 2. Now turn the deck assembly upside down and check the duct leading to the hood for lint or obstructions. If your dryer has a soft bonnet, check the hose and hose assembly for obstructions.

Is the air duct system clear?

Yes—You have not found the fault. Proceed to Fault Symptom **10330**.

No—Clean the duct. A vacuum cleaner is helpful for this job. Proceed to Step 2.

Step 2—Assemble the dryer, plug it in, and operate the control through the full range.

Does the dryer have a normal air flow?

Yes—Fault has been found and corrected.

No—Proceed to Fault Symptom **10330**.

10330

Impeller loose

Step 1—Remove the inner case deck assembly as described in Fault Symptom **10010** Step 2. Examine the impeller to make sure it is firmly attached to the motor shaft.

Is the impeller firmly attached?

Yes—You must have overlooked something in your previous checks. Look over your work. There is an obstruction you have missed.

No—Fasten the impeller. Rotate it with your finger to make sure it moves freely and does not strike anything. Proceed to Step 2.

Step 2—Plug the dryer into an active wall outlet and rotate the switch through the full range.

Does the warm air circulate as it should?

Yes—The fault has been found and repaired.

No—Recheck your work. There is an obstruction in the line you have not noticed.

ELECTRICAL TESTING AND TEST TOOLS

SERVICE PROCEDURE 11000

Electrical Circuit Testing Tools

The home repairman will find that for most home appliance troubleshooting or tests, a simple neon tester and a flashlight circuit tester are usually the only electrical test tools needed. These test tools, shown in Figs. 23 and 26, are very inexpensive.

1. Use of a neon tester

The neon tester (Fig. 23) is simply a small neon bulb in a protective covering attached to two wire leads. These leads are insulated and are fitted with tips called probes. Neon testers can be purchased in various ratings, 115/230 volts up to 600 volts. It is advisable to buy a neon tester which is capable of testing both low, 115 to 120 volts, and up to a high of 600 volts.

For those who desire greater protection, or who are uncomfortable with the usual short leads of the neon tester, Fig. 24A shows the addition of longer lead wires on the neon tester. These longer wires should be permanently soldered or mechanically secured onto the probes of the tester and the connection wrapped tightly with electrical tape.

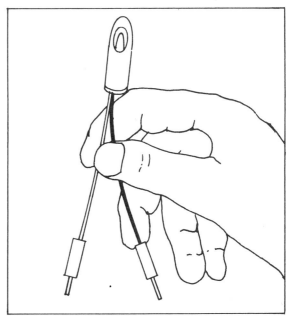

Fig. 23. Neon tester.

Use the neon tester as follows:
(a) Use only one hand if possible. Hold the tester loosely with your fingers.
(b) Spread the leads apart by holding one lead with thumb and index finger, and move the other lead with the middle finger.
(c) Touch one lead to one point in the circuit under test and the other lead to the second point. For example, the

wall utility outlet receptacle: place one lead in one slot and the other lead in the other slot. A safe way to use the tester is to use an alligator clip lead on one probe and, using one hand, slip that probe to the ground side of the circuit under test. Then, using only one hand, the other long probe can be used to safely touch other points in the circuit (see Fig. 24B).

CAUTION

BE CERTAIN TO HOLD TESTER ONLY BY INSULATED PARTS. NEVER TOUCH OR HOLD BY TIPS OR ENDS OF PROBES; USE ONE HAND TO AVOID POSSIBILITY OF ELECTROCUTION.

CAUTION

(d) When the circuit under test is LIVE, the neon lamp will illuminate. Be sure good contact is being made between the metal tip of the probe and the point on the circuit tested. A dead circuit will not light the lamp.

(e) When using the neon tester for testing a fuse in a fusebox, place one probe on the ground and the other probe on one side of the fuse. The lamp should glow if the fuse is good. If it does not, place the probe on the other side of the fuse. If the lamp glows on the hot side, but not the opposite side of the fuse (the side going to the appliance), the fuse is bad.

(f) When using the neon tester to check a LIVE switch, i.e., a switch which has live electricity going through it, place one probe on one terminal of the switch and the other probe on the other terminal of the switch. Turn switch on—lamp should glow; turn switch off—lamp should go out. If

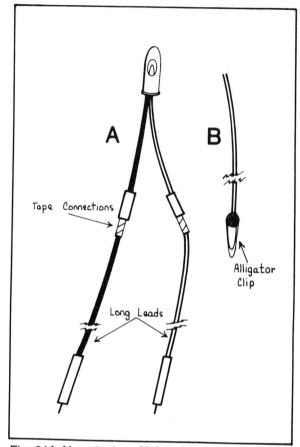

Fig. 24A. Neon tester with long leads.
Fig. 24B. Neon tester with alligator clip lead.

lamp does not glow—or stays on—the switch is bad.

2. Use of a flashlight circuit tester/lamp

A flashlight circuit tester, shown in Fig. 25A, is an ordinary battery-operated flashlight attached to two wire test leads. The cross-sectional sketch of a flashlight circuit tester, shown in Fig. 25B, shows how these two wires are connected to the case of the flashlight and to the standard "D" size battery cells inside the case. Note that the flashlight switch must be closed in order for this tester to work. Always check this switch before use. This tester is absolutely safe from electrical hazards under proper use.

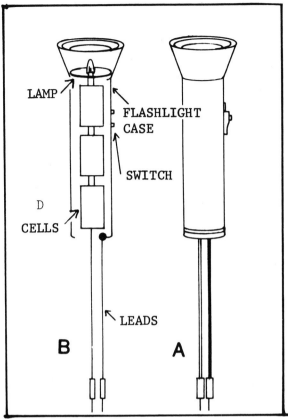

Fig. 25A. Flashlight circuit tester.
Fig. 25B. Cross-sectional sketch of flashlight circuit tester.

CAUTION

NEVER USE A FLASHLIGHT TESTER IN A LIVE CIRCUIT. ALWAYS SHUT POWER OFF FIRST.

CAUTION

The flashlight circuit tester is used as follows for continuity testing:

(a) Using the tester to check the continuity of a switch:
1. Isolate the switch terminals. If necessary, remove one terminal lead to be sure the switch is isolated from the circuit.
2. Place flashlight circuit tester across the two switch terminals. Make sure tester is ON.
3. Open and close the switch under test.
4. When the switch being tested is closed the flashlight should light; when the switch is off the light should be out. Any variation means the switch is defective.

(b) Using the tester to check cordset (Fig. 26).
1. Connect the tester to plug end and receptacle end as shown. Turn tester ON.
2. If tester does not light, switch one lead of tester to other plug prong so as to check 1A with 2A, etc.
3. If tester still does not light, cord is defective.

Fig. 26

REPAIR TOOLS

Most of the tools needed to repair small appliances are those which most people already own. Refer to Figs. 27–30 to see if there may be one or two additional tools you may need.

Figure 27 shows two types of soldering irons and a propane torch.

SERVICE PROCEDURE 12000

Figure 28 shows regular pliers (A), needle-nose (B), and cutting (C). A wire stripping tool (A) is shown in Fig. 30, and a visegrip (B) in Fig. 30.

Refer to Service Procedure **11000** for a probe test light.

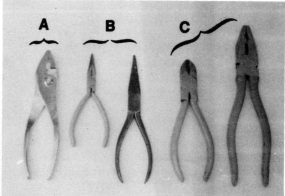

Fig. 28

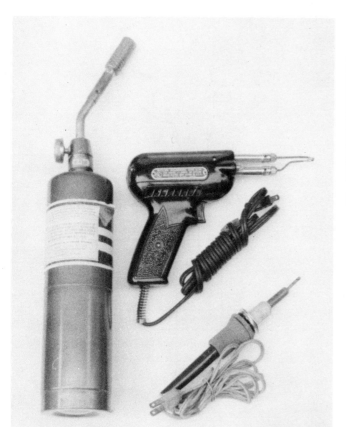

Fig. 27

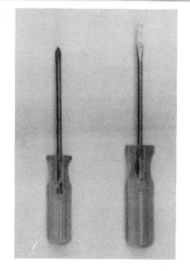

Fig. 29

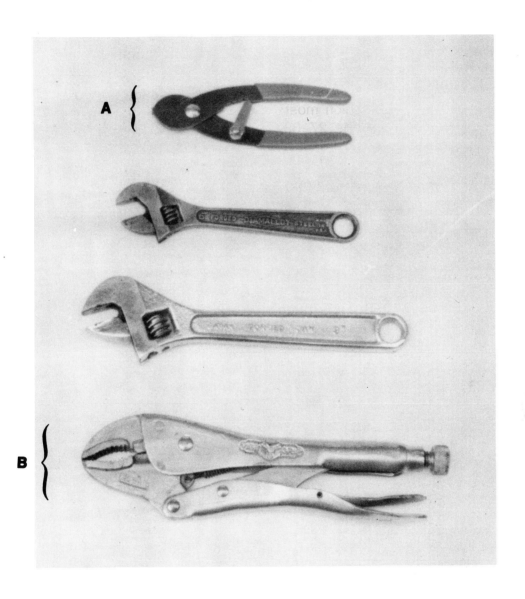

Fig. 30

INDEX

Fault symptom numbers are in boldface type; page numbers are in lightface type.

Bitter coffee, **1300,** 20
Blockage in pump assembly, **1110,** 15
Blower, **9200–40,** 87–89
Boiling coffee, **1100–40,** 15–17
Broiler, electric oven
  does not reach maximum temperature at high
    setting, **7100–20,** 69–70
  will not heat, **7000–30,** 64–68
Broiler/rotisserie
  does not reach maximum temperature, **8100,**
    74
  motor does not operate, **8200–30,** 75–77
  will not heat, **8000–20,** 72–73

Calrod heating element, **7030,** 67–68, **8020,** 73
Circuit testing tools, **11000,** 103–105
Cleaning fluids, **4040,** 44
Cleaning percolators, **1300,** 20
Clothes irons, dry
  will not heat, **5000–30,** 48–51
Clothes irons, steam, 53
  heat cannot be adjusted **6100–20,** 55
  leaks, **6200–30,** 56–58
  no or poor spray, **6400–20,** 61
  produces little or no steam, **6300–20,** 59–60
  will not heat, **6000,** 54
Coffee Makers(non-submersible)
  bitter, **1300,** 20
  boils or repercolates, **1100–40,** 15–17
  does not stay warm after brewing, **1400–20,** 21
  weak, **1200–20,** 18–19
  will not heat, **1000–40,** 8–14
Connections, loose, service procedure, **1020,** 10
Connectors, thermostat, **1030,** 10, 13
Control knob
  fry pans, **3110,** 36
  hair dryer, **10010,** 93–94
  space heater, **9010,** 80–81

  steam irons, **6110,** 55
Control shaft, stuck, **3210,** 37
Control unit
  electric ovens, **7120,** 69–70
  griddles and grills, **4030,** 43–44, **4120,** 46
Cord, defective
  coffee makers, **1010,** 8–9
  corn poppers, **2010,** 24, 26
  griddles and grills, **4010,** 40–42
  space heater, **9010,** 80–81
Cord set, defective
  broiler/rotisserie, **8010,** 72–73 **8210,** 75–76
  clothes irons, dry, **5010,** 49
  clothes irons, steam, **6000,** 54
  electric oven, **7010,** 64–65
  fry pans, **3010,** 32, 34
  hair dryer, **10010,** 93–94
Corn poppers
  overheats, burns corn, will not turn off, **2100,**
    29
  will not heat, **2000–40,** 24–28
  will not pop, **2200–20,** 30

Dryer, hair
  heating element works but motor does not,
    10100–30, 96–97
  runs but does not heat, **10200–30,** 98–100
  warm air does not enter the hood, **10300–30,**
    101–102
  will not heat and motor is inoperative,
    10000–30, 92–95

Electrical testing, **11000,** 103–105
Electric oven/broiler
  does not reach maximum temperature at high
    setting, **7100–20,** 69–70
  will not heat, **7000–30,** 64–68

Fan blade, loose, **9210,** 87
Filter, fouled, **10310,** 101
Flashlight circuit tester/lamp, **11000,** 104–105
Fry pans
does not get hot enough, **3100–20,** 36
overheats, **3200–20,** 37
will not heat, **3000–30,** 32–35

Griddles
cleaning, **4040,** 44
does not fully heat at high setting, **4100–20,** 45–46
will not heat, **4000–40,** 40–44
Grills
cleaning, **4040,** 44
does not fully heat at high setting, **4100–20,** 45–46
will not heat, **4000–40,** 40–44

Hair dryer
heater element works but motor does not work, **10100–30,** 96–97
runs but does not heat, **10200–30,** 98–100
warm air does not enter the hood, **10300–30,** 101–102
will not heat and motor is inoperative, **10000–30,** 92–95
Heat duct or hose, plugged, **10320,** 101
Heater, space
blower does not work, **9200–40,** 87–89
does not reach maximum temperature, **9100–20,** 85–86
will not heat, **9000–50,** 80–84
Heater well, fouled, **1210,** 18
Heating element
broiler/rotisserie, **8020,** 73, **8110,** 74
clothes irons, dry, **5030,** 51
clothes irons, steam, **6000,** 54
coffee makers, **1040,** 13–14
corn poppers, **2040,** 28, **2220,** 30
electric oven, **7030,** 66–68, **7100–20,** 69–70
fry pans, **3030,** 35
griddles and grills, **4040,** 44, **4110,** 45–46
hair dryer, **10230,** 99–100
space heater, **9040,** 82–83, **9110,** 85
Hood, warm air does not enter, **10300–30,** 101–102
Hot element, not tight or flush with base, **1120,** 15–16

Impeller
jammed, **10110,** 96
loose, **10330,** 102
Insulation, **1020,** 10
Internal wire, defective
coffee makers, **1020,** 9–10
corn poppers, **2020,** 26–27
griddles and grills, **4020,** 42–43
hair dryer, **10120,** 96, **10210,** 98–99
space heater, **9020,** 81–82, **9220,** 87–88
Irons, dry
will not heat, **5000–30** 48–51
Irons, steam
heat cannot be adjusted, **6100–20,** 55
leaks, **6200–30,** 56–58
no or poor spray, **6400–20,** 61
produces little or no steam, **6300–20,** 59–60
will not heat, **6000,** 54

"Keeps Hot" element, defective, **1130,** 16, **1420,** 21

Leaks in irons, **6200–30,** 56–58

Motor
hair dryer, **10030,** 95, **10130,** 96–97
rotisserie, **8230,** 76–77
space heater, **9240,** 88–89
Neon tester, **11000,** 103–104
Nichrome wire, **7030,** 66–67
Nozzle assembly, defective, **6420,** 61
Nozzle orifice, plugged, **6410,** 61

Oven/broiler, electric
does not reach maximum temperature at high setting, **7100–20,** 69–70
will not heat, **7000–30,** 64–68
Overheating
coffee makers, **1100–40,** 15–17
corn poppers, **2100,** 29
fry pans, **3200–20,** 37

Power cord, defective
broiler/rotisserie, **8010,** 72–73, **8210,** 75–76
clothes irons, dry, **5010,** 49
clothes irons, steam, **6000,** 54
coffee makers, **1010,** 8–9
corn poppers, **2010,** 24, 26

electric oven, **7010,** 64–65
fry pans, **3010,** 32, 34
griddles and grills, **4010,** 40–42
hair dryer, **10010,** 93–94
space heater, **9010,** 80–81
Pump assembly, defective, **1110,** 15, **6420,** 61

Release valve, defective, **6220,** 57
Repair tools, **12000,** 106–107
Repercolating coffee, **1100,** 15–17
Reservoir leaks, steam iron, **6230,** 57–58
Rotisserie
cleaning, **8200,** 75
does not reach maximum temperature, **8100,** 74
motor does not operate, **8200–30,** 75–77
will not heat, **8000–20,** 72–73

Solder, silver, **2020,** 26–27, **5020,** 51
Space heater
blower does not work, **9200–40,** 87–89
does not reach maximum temperature, **9100–20,** 85–86
will not heat, **9000–50,** 80–84
Spray, iron, **6400–20,** 61
Steam chamber leaks, iron, **6210,** 56–57
Steam control, **6320,** 59–60
Steam irons, **6000–400,** 53–61
Steam ports, plugged, **6310,** 59
Steam, producing little or no, **6300–20,** 59–60
Switch, defective
hair dryer, **10020,** 94, **10220,** 99
rotisserie motor, **8220,** 76
space heater, **9230,** 88

Temperature control unit

electric oven, **7010,** 64–65, **7020,** 65–66, **7120,** 69–70
griddles and grills, **4030,** 43–44, **4120,** 46
Terminal pins, **2020,** 26
Thermostat
clothes irons, dry, **5020,** 49–51
clothes irons, steam, **6000,** 54, **6120,** 55
coffee makers, **1030,** 10–13, **1140,** 16–17, **1220,** 18–19, **1400,** 21
corn poppers, **2030,** 27–28, **2100,** 29, **2210,** 30
electric oven, **7020,** 65–66
fry pans, **3020,** 34–35, **3120,** 36, **3220,** 37
griddles and grills, **4030,** 43–44, **4120,** 46
space heater, **9030,** 82, **9120,** 85–86
"Tired" heating element
broiler/rotisserie, **8110,** 74
electric oven, **7100–20,** 69–70
griddles and grills, **4110,** 45–46
Tools
electrical test, **11000,** 103–105
repair, **12000,** 106–107

Valve stem on steam control, inoperative, **6320,** 59–60
Valve, water release, **6220,** 57

Water release valve, defective, **6220,** 57
Water temperature adjustment, **1220,** 18–19
Weak coffee, **1200,** 18–19
Wire connection, internal
coffee makers, **1020,** 9–10
corn poppers, **2020,** 26–27
griddles and grills, **4020,** 42–43
hair dryer, **10120,** 96, **10210,** 98–99
space heater, **9020,** 81–82, **9220,** 87–88
Wire leaf, replacement, **2020,** 26–27